BAD MINDS, HIGH PLACES

Ohio to Washington State

The FBI Raids
on Cleveland

America's Archipelago of Legal Failure

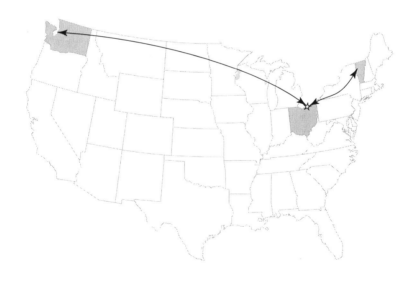

Robert Grundstein
Stowe, Vermont

Dedicated to Professor Maris Wolff
and
the 158,000 people under 18 who left Cleveland
in the past decade

Maris teaches dance and a standard of conscience
The others taught us when to leave

Forward

The Carnival of Failure

"…the great possessions of the missions are given over to be preyed upon by the harpies of the civil power, who are sent there in the capacity of administradores, to settle up the concerns; and who usually end, in a few years, by making themselves fortunes, and leaving their stewardships worse than they found them." R. Henry Dana, "Two Years Before the Mast".

When a litigant goes to court, he shouldn't have to worry that a judge or prosecutor's first concern is the risk or benefit to him/herself of determining a case a certain way. But in a politicized judiciary, that's exactly what happens. Adam Liptak of the "New York Times" did an article on the Ohio Supreme Court and found that Justice O'Donnell voted in favor of his significant contributors 91% of the time.

Bedford Municipal Court is Running a Whore House

Bedford Ohio Municipal Court Judge Harry Jacobs and the Law Director, Ken Schuman, were just indicted for promoting prostitution and other crimes. Ex Bedford Judge Peter Junkin, was found to have arranged jobs in his court for women who provided sex to former County Commissioner Jim Dimora in exchange for employment.

We've approached an emergency state in which legal decisions not only prioritize professional well-being, assets and unfair advantage , but are used by those entrusted with our ethical system to conduct crime. It's not limited to Cleveland. The civil forfeitures practiced in Texas and elsewhere are asset transfers arranged by willing police, prosecutors and judges. See "Taken" in the August 12-19th 2013 "New Yorker" magazine. Arizona had a massive misappropriation of power. The FBI worked with special investigators to break up a cartel run by Maricopa County (Phoenix) Prosecutor Andrew Thomas and Sheriff Joe Arpaio (yes, That Joe Arpaio) designed to control the judiciary and law enforcement. Thomas and Arpaio even formed a "Maricopa Anti-Corruption Enforcement" unit, (MACE), which they used to intimidate people who weren't corrupt. Two judges in Luzerne County, Pennsylvania were bribed to commit juveniles to private detention centers. Corruption is worst in the states where judges are elected.

The legal system has to be approached with an informed model. Innocent parties think it's a place where financially comfortable judges make studied and fair decisions. It's not. The judiciary can act as an interest group which favors partisan relations, prioritizes its own tenure and commits significant intellectual and character failures. It's filled with conventionalists who want to say what everyone else is saying.

Litigants should regard the legal system as an operating set of prioritized relations in which parties to a suit are entitled to benefits on a disproportionate basis. Our jurisprudence has become corporatized and directed toward individual and small group advantage.

The dirty battle of law suits is a fight for the record and to generate an order which carries the presumption of legitimacy. It's a competition to establish "legal fact". People describe the truth in terms of empiricism (sensory data) and rationalism, or deductive inferences from facts. There's a third description of "truth" which has to do with neither. "Truth" is something that has environmental significance. It's the thing on which people act. "Legal Fact" is in that 3rd category. In Cleveland and other jurisdictions, it's common to use an unfair advantage to contrive orders based on perjury or insufficient evidence. Once an order is recorded it will be enforced by the police power which is all that matters. You can spend the rest of your life explaining the lie foisted upon you and no one will care. The enforceable record is the fact.

We're in an age of shortage now. The 3rd world America used to exploit became the 1st world. N. Europeans compete with Indians, Chinese and Koreans for energy and natural resources. The tawny people have weapons, trade revenue and manufacturing economies. Over the past 40 years, American poor got poorer, the middle class shrank and huge wealth has become even more disproportionately concentrated in a small group of people. The public sector is left for those who can't afford to avoid it. Education became privatized for the middle class. Class differences even between white people have become exaggerated.

In an age of economic uncertainty and social deterioration, the notion that people have intrinsic value is harder to maintain. The cost of morality has become too high and uncertain. The idea of a national social contract and responsible use of advantage become quaint relics. Just get something for your group at the expense of other Americans who aren't as important. Utilitarian relations become preferred and utility actually will become the equivalent of moral and ethical thought. It's a confusing lie the human mind is designed to tell itself.

Fascism doesn't necessarily involve shrill rhetoric, mass rallies and concentration camps. It is a form of corporatism in which legal, economic and political power is concentrated among a small group of people and exercised in favor of that small group.

Author Morris Berman believes America is shifting from a Republic to an empire; from a nation to a state in decline. There is reason to agree with him. Americans conduct personal relations like business relations, the family is not a reliable structure, the innocence of youth is at risk in public schools and we treat our elderly in an appalling fashion. The American superego is gone. We live in an emotional void.

Table of Contents

1

The News from Ohio
What First Amendment Is That?

"Don't be stupid. Judges and police are an interest group. You can't rely on right and wrong…it's group maintenance and income. Moralists get killed, alone, in the dark." My Dad…to me.

The phone rang in Vermont. It was 7:30 Halloween night, 2007.

"Hi, this is Lt. Tonnelli of the Solon, Ohio police department. I'm looking for a Mr. Robert Grundstein".

I said that was me.

"We have a complaint from a judge's wife that you were seen on their property last night."

That's odd. Seemed like your basic lie. I hadn't been to Cleveland since the prior April, when I published an editorial I wrote about former Bedford, Ohio judge, Peter Junkin. He ruined a case of mine and I passed out a criticism against him on the steps of his courthouse during business hours. I sued the management of a Cleveland condominium I owned for fraud. It charged $150,000.00 for a roof that only cost $76,000.00. Junkin had the case and dismissed the action at a hearing in Ohio for which I drove from Vermont.

It should have been an easy case but Junkin conducted it as if I was a proven offender. He wasn't concerned by the embezzled amounts and regarded me as a bothersome perpetrator. The hearing was like a scene from the movie "Red Corner" in which the Chinese judge was instructed by "powerful interests" to convict Richard Gere. Junkin wasn't prepared and tried to learn the file by flipping pages on the bench, while muttering criticisms of phrases he didn't like in my brief. He started the hearing with, "Mr. Grundstein, you must think I'm really stupid". I did, but it was still frightening. Violence was a latent presence in his courtroom.

He was incompetent, emotionally uncertain and shamelessly partisan to local counsel. I wanted to expose a representative of a failed system that elects judges on the basis of politicized relations and insufficient screening. That feeling was confirmed two years later when the FBI raided Cleveland and Junkin was subpoenaed for alleged mob affiliations.

"Sorry, I haven't been there. Must be some mistake".

"Well, thank you Mr. Grundstein. We just have to check on complaints. Have a good evening".

45 minutes later, the Vermont State Police knocked. I opened the door to find an officer standing 5 feet from the threshold along the exterior wall in a manner to avoid gunshots. I know the Vt. State police. I helped them with an undercover drug investigation concerning some of my tenants who were involved with methamphetamine.

There were two of them; Officer Julie Hammond and a man.

"Hi, Bob, mind if we come in?

"No, not at all. What's up?

"Well, we have a warrant for your extradition to Ohio. You're charged with a 2nd degree felony. You'll have to stop cooking your dinner and come with us."

I turned off the stove and listened to the cooking sounds of my meat wane. They took a set of handcuffs from a belt and apologized for the necessary security. I presented my hands forward. I didn't know how to do this. They grinned and apologized again.

"Sorry, your hands have to go behind".

This was depressing. Julie Hammond was good looking. I finally get a scenario with her involving handcuffs but I was headed to a cell in isolation. I hoped my next sexual contact wouldn't include "Bubba the Love Sponge".

We drove past landscape that had been domestic to me for over 35 years. The benevolence of this place and our lives had never seen police. This was something that happened in another, entirely different, existential matrix. I went to the University of Michigan. My father was a professor of law and advanced management. Our friends were judges and law teachers. Criminals were furtive outsiders.

I was taken to a holding cell in the Morrisville State Police Barracks. Morrisville is a small merchant community that served the timber, farming and asbestos economy of the region. I was now a captive in an anachronistic and benign setting. Somebody or a group of somebodies in Ohio was removing the innocence from the prior 35 years of my life. Some secret force acting under the police power 1/3 of a continent away, was misappropriating my life.

The cell was really a caged area in a larger room with equipment to process prisoners. It was very quiet and not unpleasant. The fluorescent lighting was subdued and cast shadows in the room corners. The officer in charge was cordial and made it a point to diminish the emotional character of the event. I was completely alone and didn't have to worry about other prisoners. The handcuffs were taken off and I sat quietly in this holding area. I was told the state prosecutor was being contacted to approve the warrant of extradition. I was allowed to bring a book and read for an hour and a half.

The silence was interrupted when the arresting officer came and announced the local prosecutor said Ohio didn't provide enough evidence to hold me in Vermont. This made complete sense. I was driven back and invited the officer in. He sat down and thanked me for being so cooperative. He also warned me that the indictment in Ohio was still active and the state could correct any defects in its request to Vermont, after which this process could repeat itself. I went to bed and noticed a new sepia tone of menace coloring my vision. It remained for the next 12 months.

I called an attorney in Ohio who specialized in criminal matters. He confirmed what the Vermont State Trooper said. Defects in warrants were not *res judicata* and could be corrected.

Five days later, a huge State Trooper arrived and said I'd have to go with him. He knew me from the past. He was one of the Vermont State Police who asked for help with some of my tenants who were suspected of trafficking in methamphetamine and crack. They asked me to do some undercover investigation and contrive to enter the rental premises for evidence. I was terrified, but did what I could. I was working with four troopers, two of whom were undercover agents. When I asked what would happen if I was shot or targeted by Hell's Angels, the police promised they would make a note of it.

This connection served me well. On the way over to the local holding cell, the officer showed me evidence on which Ohio relied. It claimed an event in April of 2003. I had ATM receipts to prove I wasn't in Ohio before, during or after that time. I was in New Hampshire and Vermont. The officer stared at me as I laughed in recognition of the elaborate falsehood which had been organized against me. Someone in Ohio had mobilized the police and Judiciary of two states.

We repeated the booking process in the Morrisville holding cell except this time I was fingerprinted. When I asked what was next, Sgt. Campbell told me we'd go to a bail hearing before a judge and the prosecutor. It was held the same afternoon.

I was brought to a Vermont County court for the bail hearing in a strange apparatus. Handcuffs are attached by short metal chains to a five inch leather belt with a substantial buckle. Your arms become vestigial limbs in which yours hands can flip about for limited purposes. I couldn't reach the table to write or reach anything. Sgt. Greg Campbell did everything he could to make me comfortable. He phoned an attorney of my choice who was available and came right over. The three of us met in an ante-chamber across from the main courtroom. It had tall ceilings and windows designed to express an austere, abstract, New England notion of elegance. Even on gray days, the room was illuminated.

I explained my happenstance to the attorney, who hadn't had a chance to read anything about this case. Sgt. Campbell apologized for having to stay in the room. I told him I wanted him to remain because I wanted everyone possible to know what was taking place. I was being chased across 1/3 of a country for exercising my 1st Amendment rights.

We were brought before Judge Brian Grearson and a bunch of other people I had never seen before. It was very precipitous. Three hours ago I was fooling around with my car in the driveway. The state prosecutor sat at a table to our side. The state asked for $50,000.00 bond. Since I had no experience with this, I didn't know that you have to have cash for bail prior to hearing or you will be taken to jail where you don't have access to a bank. The police will not take you to an ATM. At 10%, I would have had to pay $5,000.00. No one except drug dealers carry this amount on a daily basis.

My attorney was quick witted and explained that since I was a bar member, I was an officer of the court and not a flight risk. I had no priors and had been connected to the community for 30 years. The judge agreed and set bail at $10,000.00. I had to provide $1000.00 or go to jail. I asked my attorney for $1000.00. He grimaced. Sgt. Campbell asked if I had any other ideas. I told him of an attorney friend in Burlington who would provide the money. Sgt. Campbell called for me and left a message.

I was led from the courtroom and out the side door to the adjoining police station. The policeman in charge of court security was a friend. He waved sadly and called good luck to me. Sgt. Campbell made it a point of having me sit in the front seat so anyone who saw me wouldn't know I was being arrested. We listened to the radio station of my choice and he called my friend in Burlington again. It was late afternoon and people were between work and home. We drove up and down the cute curved hills of Morrisville to a location outside of Hardwick, where I was passed to another officer. We drove through country which was part of my life and which for a generation was only characterized by benevolence and virtue. The officer offered me part of his granola bar and wanted to know what radio station I liked. He also called my attorney to make sure someone could get me out of jail that night. He kept getting the voice mail. Sgt. Campbell called my friend a third time to make sure we left a message.

Police can make things very easy or very difficult. There is a surprising amount of discretion they can exercise to make detention oppressive and stigma laden or give it the characteristic of an anomalous event which entails inconvenience but a manageable resolution. We stopped in the gravel parking area of a closed restaurant in Hardwick. It was a remote area with hills and tundra-like grasslands. Pictures of moose adorn the road signs. The beginning of November can be surprisingly warm in Vermont and comfortable winds moved the grass in dense waves. Sgt. Campbell left the car and spoke with the second trooper for a long time. I was going to St. Johnsbury which is a medium security prison. I sat in the car and watched them speak.

When they were done, Sgt. Campbell actually introduced me to the second state trooper who made it a point to be friendly. He apologized for having to cuff my hands behind my back and have me sit in the back seat this time, but chose to exercise this protocol. During the ride he turned to me several times to ask if I was O.K.. He turned on the radio and asked if I liked the station. We reached the medium security prison in St. Johnsbury, after a half hour and went in the front. It was dark by now.

I expected to be appropriated by a contingent of over-sized guards and subject to an introduction designed to intimidate a new arrival. It wasn't like that at all.

The staff couldn't have been nicer. They helped me with new procedures like blowing into something that registered chemical substances. My cuffs were removed and I was brought to a large desk near the glass doors of the main entrance. A bearded man presided and showed me some paper work I had to fill out. He was more like a social worker than what I imagined a prison guard would be. His manner was kind and solicitous. He chuckled when I didn't know what to do with the exhaler they use to measure drug levels in new arrivals and said reassuring things. More people came in after me. A woman who had been arrested several times before was re-entered into the prison. She was greeted like a neighbor or other acquaintance. The staff expressed concern about her recurring pneumonia. Bologna sandwiches and a vividly colored beverage were distributed.

I was moved to a smallish cell with 2 other people who were going to be moved. They were non-violent guys in their mid-twenties, one of whom transported himself to the prison after the hiatus between sentencing and incarceration. Some people are allowed to stay home during this interval if they promise to present themselves at prison on a certain date. We all talked and ate bologna sandwiches. I was definitely the odd-man but felt no hostility. The guy who just turned himself in seemed unconcerned and cheerful. He was French and rogue handsome with black hair and a mustache. He was chatty and engaged everyone. His manner included self-irony and he told us of the special meals his sisters made for him the weekend before he had to leave. I got the impression this was a family ritual known among a certain risk-pool in Vermont. Our other cellmate was subdued and less optimistic. No one discussed why we were here. I assumed it was bad manners to ask. We were removed one at a time at which point we all wished one another good luck.

I was moved once again to a larger cell directly in front of the intake desk. I guess the more reliable your release seemed, the closer you got to the exit. Another form had to be filled out and I was asked more questions by a person at the desk. These included details of my professional life. The dialogue took place across a corridor where an inmate mopping the floors commented on my status as an attorney. I assumed this would be publicized to 400 inmates within a half hour.

An attorney friend drove over and bailed me out. It was so good to see his Latinized presence. His narrow features and beret made him look like my Basque rescue team. This was a major favor. It was a long drive and late at night. Plus, he had to lend me $1000.00. The intricately timed exchange of papers and custody release was performed by a senior corrections officer I hadn't seen before. I was driven home and lit the wood stove.

The next morning I stopped into the local market and noticed a "Wanted-Fugitive" poster with my name on it. It was stapled to the community bulletin board facing the road. Everybody knew.

I proceeded to draft my own writ of *habeas corpus* and prepare for additional Vermont hearings.

From this time on, I was subject to all orders of the local District court. I had to appear when it said to appear and could not leave the state without permission. A case management hearing was scheduled for two weeks later. I could present my Writ of *Habeas Corpus* then.

2

Extradition and the Great Writ

"You're going to love Ohio"

I accumulated a history of my case and found the Ohio Grand Jury returned a "No Bill" against my indictment. That should have been decisive. The police can't go back again with the same evidence. Only 4% of Grand Jury decisions return a No Bill.

A Grand Jury is responsible for criminal indictments in Ohio. The Grand Jury system is one sided and designed to indict anyone who comes before it. NY State Chief Justice Solomon Wachtler said "you could indict a ham sandwich". It's a truly defective way to find fault. In most states, the Grand Jury is secret and evidence is presented by state law enforcement. A defendant has no idea he has been targeted and is not even present. He has no notice that this thing is being planned against him. On the other hand, the state may present its case on a unilateral basis with as many witnesses as it wants.

Grand Jurors are assigned like other jurors and must sit unless legally excused. Their term varies from jurisdiction to jurisdiction, but in Cuyahoga County, Ohio, they are summoned two days a week for four months and will hear 80 to 100 cases a day. The jury will only hear police, prosecutors, detectives and other witnesses testifying on behalf of the prosecution. There is no attorney for defense. It is a secret, *in camera* proceeding. There are about five minutes to decide each case and the indictment rate is around 96 percent. The jury will return either a "True Bill", meaning there is probable cause to prosecute, or a "No Bill" meaning there is not sufficient evidence for arrest. Witness names are confidential.

Some states, like Hawaii, have modified Grand Jury practices. A suspect is notified of a Grand Jury hearing and he is allowed to attend with an attorney. In Ohio, however, there is no accountability. It's a liar's factory and perfect for a corrupt police force and judiciary to practice vendettas and illegal agendas.

Over time, I accumulated details of the process against me. The Cleveland detective who testified against me was named Mackey, and worked for County Sheriff Gerald McFaul. Sheriff McFaul was arrested, tried and convicted on federal corruption charges two years later. The Grand Jury returned a "No Bill" in my favor. This should have ended the case since re-presentment with the same evidence is illegal.

Felony arraignments are heard in Cuyahoga County Court of Common Pleas. An arraignment is when an indicted party first hears the charges against him and makes a plea. Common pleas are "guilty", "not guilty" or "*no lo contendere*". "*No lo*" admits the facts but does not argue the status of guilty or not guilty. Under some circumstances, the prosecution will offer a lower penalty for a plea of "*no lo*" because it won't have to prove and litigate a case. At the time, between 15,000 and 20,000 people per year were being indicted in Cleveland. The county prosecutor was Bill Mason who had been in office for about 10 years. After another ten years, everyone in Cleveland will have been arrested.

I called a special Court Liaison for accused people in Cuyahoga County Court of Common Pleas and spoke with a representative. I told him I wasn't in Cleveland at the time and any statute of limitations had expired. He promised to consult with people above him and told me to call him back in a week. He also gave me the names of several defense attorneys. I called one of them and told her what happened. She listened in silence and promised to call after she consulted with her firm. All work was accepted or refused on a consensus basis. Her manner was polite and vacuous. I waited 4 days and called her back. Her firm refused to take the case. I called another attorney who also refused. He said the case didn't make sense and didn't want to say anything else. A third attorney wasn't sure if he wanted the case but was nice enough to give me instructions on how to approach Cleveland. The county is run by commissioners with authority inside different organizations. I was told to call the bail commissioner for the county court system.

A week later I called the Court Liaison. He spoke with a Mr. Dowling who felt there was reason to dismiss my case. Mr. Dowling had to consult with people higher up who at the time were unnamed but included Bill Mason and his first assistant, Michael O'Malley. Michael's brother was the county recorder, Pat O'Malley. Pat was Mason's college roommate.

There were other O'Malleys in the Cleveland justice system; J. Kathleen O'Malley of the N. Ohio Federal District court, Prosecutor Joe O'Malley, Joe's sister Judge Kathleen O'Malley of Common Pleas, (yes, there are two Kathleen O'Malleys) Joe's other sister, Bridget O'Malley who worked in a county job and Joe's brother, Judge Thomas O'Malley. Joe's Dad was a local attorney with a reputation as an excessive lush.

Joe and Pat later went on to jail. Bridget was fired for falsifying her time records. She attended work about half the time for which she was paid.

The bail commissioner was an affable person named Bob Prosub. I was surprised that he was personally available when I called. He asked for the case number and looked up the docket. I explained that I wasn't in Ohio on or even near the time alleged and this must be some mistake. Bob made studying noises over the phone and said;

"What's this? You got a "No Bill" from the Grand Jury. (Only about 4% of all parties before a Grand Jury get a "No Bill"). No one gets a "No Bill". It means a very weak case. This doesn't seem right. Here's what you do. Unless you get dismissed, you'll have to come in for arraignment. Do NOT come in this month. The judges rotate. You have to avoid this guy McGinty who is assigned to arraignments this month. He is a real trip. Wait until J. John Russo is on the bench. Now, another thing, Do NOT go to the first floor or turn yourself into the police. Go upstairs and sign in at the courtroom. Otherwise, you'll be put in jail immediately and held until the arraignment. I'll recommend that you be released on your personal recognizance. You won't have to post bond. You should have no trouble. They always take the bail commissioner's recommendation. Strange stuff goes on in this county."

I was encouraged by a stranger in the court system. Bob's help provided warm comfort and reason to believe in a fair resolution. He saw and confirmed my suspicions. In the meantime, I had to appear before a Vermont judge for release of restraints by way of *Habeas Corpus*, or further instructions on what restraints would be imposed for the future.

I called an attorney to ask about extradition. He said buses are used. It's not like a taxi or police car where you are taken directly to a destination. Extradition buses have routes and accumulate prisoners across several states. If I was extradited from Vermont, I might have to endure a trip extending across Vermont, New York, Pennsylvania, Virginia, Tennessee, Kentucky and Ohio. It could take two weeks. Did I want to remain chained in a bus with 60 felons, subject to an unsupervised transportation staff? I looked on the internet about these transport companies.

The buses were unmarked and the windows were obscured. It was like being moved about in a light armored vehicle. I didn't like the milieu and hoped for better alternatives.

My Very Own *Habeas Corpus*

During the next 2 weeks, I prepared for the Vermont hearing at which my state restraint would be ended or continued until extradition took place. The document I had to prepare is a famous writ known as *Habeas Corpus*. It means, "You Have the Body" and directs a restraining authority to produce the body (prisoner) and show a reason why the prisoner or party subject to restraints (limitations on interstate travel are also included as "restraints) should not be released. *Habeas* takes place in a Show Cause hearing in which the presumption is that a person should not be held unless the state can give a good reason to continue holding that party. The presumption in a Writ of *Habeas* is that the prisoner should go free and the state has the burden of proving a Constitutional right to continue restraint.

Habeas Corpus is known as "The Great Writ" and has its historical roots in the *Magna Carta*. *Habeas Corpus* is fundamental to American and all other English common law systems of jurisprudence. It is a direct remedy for adjudicating the conditions of restraint. *Magna Carta* makes reference to *Habeas Corpus* through express reference to "the law of the land". The exact quote is: "...no free man shall be taken or imprisoned or disseised or exiled or in any way destroyed except by the lawful judgment of their peers or by the law of the land." The practice of *Habeas Corpus* was settled practice and law at the time of *Magna Carta* and was thus was included as a fundamental part of the unwritten common "law of the land" as recognized by the *Magna Carta*.

Writs represent something very important about the American legal system. There are many writs in addition to *Habeas Corpus*. They include *Prohibition*, *Mandamus*, *Quo Warranto*, *Procedendo*, *Certiorari* and *Coram Nobis*. Writs were traditionally appeals to ecclesiastical or religious courts (Courts of the Chancellor) which co-existed with secular courts and were designed to give relief against inequitable and under-informed application of written law. It was a chance for a party to say, "Yeah, the written rule is clear, but it's not right to apply it in this circumstance."

Writs are Equitable in nature and ask an authority to remember and apply a culture of ethical and moral thought of which the written law is just evidence. "Equity follows the law" is a phrase which expresses the duty of judges to recognize that they must interpret the law in a manner consistent with our ethical, moral and Constitutional culture. The culture and jurisprudence of a legal system is more important than the unexamined application of its written laws. *"Summum jus, summa injuria"*; which basically means un-interpreted, written law only provides injury. Extreme right makes extreme injury.

The "Law-Equity" distinction is a fundamental part of American jurisprudence. The U.S. maintained separate courts of Law and Equity until they merged in 1938, but the different character of law and equity is still recognized.

Magna Carta and *Habeas* all sound very noble, but one must remember that English lords had to force King John to sign the *Magna Carta* under threat of violence. John later tried to retract the document. All of which proves the evolution of rights is not a straight line of progress and that there is always some son of a bitch willing to turn on his word. Joe Stalin was right; "no man, no problem".

Preparing my own writ was odd. I felt like I was engraving my own tombstone. My arguments were strong. Extradition is a peculiar business with many moving parts. There is the "asylum" state, where a defendant has been found and the "demanding" or "receiving" state which asks the asylum state to send the defendant to it. The demanding state sends a warrant of extradition to the asylum state which has *habeas* and other proceedings to see if the asylum state has enough legal basis to continue restraint against a defendant. If enough evidence is found, a Governor's Warrant will be issued and the demanding state has authority to remove a defendant to the demanding state.

Extradition law is precise. A Extradition Warrant must state that the defendant was in the demanding state at the time a crime was committed and later fled that state. Vermont and federal law is very clear, if a party can prove that he was not in the demanding state, then he must be released in the holding state. See, "Hyatt v. People, ex rel: Corkran", 188 U.S. 691; *"Defendant will be discharged with clear and satisfactory evidence that he was outside demand state at the time of the crime."*

The problem with a law can be getting a judge to enforce it. I wasn't in Ohio at the time alleged. I wasn't in Ohio the year before or the year after. My ATM receipts proved I was in Vermont and New Hampshire the months before, after and on the day I was alleged to have been in Ohio. The indictment also claimed that I altered an original document in the possession of the Court Clerk in a small suburban court. That means I went behind the bullet proof glass and electronically bolted door of that office and changed the content of an original file . . . During the day . . . In a small office where all the employees know one another and in a building shared by the police department who would be called to arrest anyone without authorization to be there. And it wasn't discovered until 4 1/2 years later. This was clearly the product of a diseased mind or a consensus of them.

A "restrained party" (prisoner) files the Writ of *Habeas*. The defendant can be the warden of a state correctional facility or state sheriff's department and is represented by a state prosecutor. The Vermont prosecutor for this action was Joel Page and he proved to be an honorable and humane person. The more he knew of my case, the less strident were his demands. After a writ is filed, the prosecutor has a chance to make a written response and a hearing is scheduled.

Our hearing was before J. Brian Grearson who asked Mr. Page about his response to my Writ and supporting evidence. Joel said "I have none". An honest prosecutor. I assumed I was free.

The judge moved slowly and shuffled papers.

"Mr. Grundstein, are you aware of what is said about the nature of a client who represents himself?"

"Of course Your Honor, "a *pro se* representative has a fool for a client". I choose to represent myself because only I can understand the history of this case and the defective nature of legal process in Cleveland, Ohio. At this point, no one could represent me better than myself. I'm sure that this court will find my briefs are responsible and the law is fundamentally in my favor."

"Well that is your privilege. At any rate, I'm not prepared to release all restraints. I will allow the defendant to travel to Ohio by his own means for the purpose of legal process in Ohio. Defendant must stay in touch with the state prosecutor until further notice."

I wanted to know about my alibi defense. In addition, the statute on which Ohio relied only assigned felony liability to people who alter a will or who alter an original court document in the possession of a court clerk. It was impossible for me to have access to an original document if I wasn't in Cleveland. All other actions under the Ohio statute were misdemeanors with a 2 year statute of limitations. I was being prosecuted four and a half years after the alleged activity. The statute of limitations would have passed.

"Your Honor, what about my alibi and statute of limitations defenses? What about the "No Bill" rendered by the Ohio Grand Jury? Under "Hyatt v People", (see above), I have shown sufficient evidence that I was not in Ohio at the time alleged and should be released from all controls. Even Ohio couldn't convict me the first time. A "No Bill" is harder to get than a "True Bill" and Ohio does not allow a re-presentment to the Grand Jury. What about that?"

Just one week before the Cuyahoga County Sheriff's Office (detective Mackey) went to the Grand Jury against me for the second time, the Ohio State Supreme Court rendered its decision of "Froehlich v Ohio Board of Mental Health", which said a Grand Jury "No Bill" permanently terminates prosecution in favor of an accused. The issue cannot be presented again.

"Mr. Grundstein, the demanding state only has to allege that you were in Ohio at the time a crime was committed. I'm not going behind the indictment."

"Your Honor, I'm not asking you to accept obscure arguments. 'Allege' is different from 'actually being there'. Federal law is quite clear. I had to have been in the demand state at the time of the alleged offense. Legal impossibility is a defense to a warrant of extradition. My ATM receipts and statute of limitations authority establish impossibility, easily."

"Mr. Grundstein, make your arrangements with the state's attorney. I'll have my order issued within an hour. You'll get a copy in the mail. You must follow all instructions or return to jail."

I ran home and phoned Cleveland. I wanted to know what Mr. Dowling had to say. How could anyone in Ohio pursue this case? I wasn't there. It's clear.

The court liaison said Mr. Dowling consulted with "higher people" and changed his mind. The prosecutor was going forward against me.

3

Crimes of Race

"We're NOT all equal. Human character and talent doesn't vary on a genetic basis from group to group, CONDITIONS do." (advice from my father)

I was operating under a significant handicap inflicted in 2005, two years before my arrest. All the defects of Cuyahoga County were starting to work in concert.

Judge Lillian Devezin-Greene had me permanently banned from all Ohio Courts during the first case I ever filed in Ohio. This first case was filed in December of 2002. It involved a matter that was remanded to her after a successful appeal and despite the fact that an identical case, against the same defendants who were embezzling from several parties in multiple states, was being conducted in the same Court under J. Janet Burnside. The action was on behalf of a newly created, 87 year old widow who was also my mother.

Devezin-Greene was elected to the Cuyahoga County Court of Common Pleas as a democrat and was adapted to the party ethos necessary to maintain oneself and advance, prior to the FBI raids of 2008-2010. She did not finish her final term as a judge and was appointed County Recorder in 2008 by County Commissioner Jimmy DiMora who was subsequently arrested, tried and imprisoned in a Federal action for bribery.

She's primarily known for her narcissism and sub-standard intellectual products delivered after excruciating delays. Stories of her pathological temper remain under-publicized. There was, however, a television investigation to find out why she fired a white girl, without legal process, who repeated an Obama joke she heard on the radio. The girl's house went into foreclosure and she still lives on welfare. No one in the county will hire her.

Lillian's defects started over 400 years ago by virtue of a criminal slavery and forced migration inflicted on an African population that couldn't maintain itself against predatory Europeans and their African agents. How does a girl from an excluded race extricate herself from the criminal foibles of a people turned against themselves and a future in the food service industry? How do you manage to leave the most disadvantaged constituency of a dying industrial economy in Youngstown, Ohio and make your way among the enemy? An enemy who provides your only alternative because your own people couldn't build anything.

The answer was provided by her times. Ride the good will of a naive Civil Rights movement and affirmative action. Learn manners to placate white people and develop whatever relations are necessary to maintain your income. Kill your enemies and hire people you can control. Preferably people who look like you and who will protect you during their tenure and in the future. You don't have to be honest, competent, hard-working or even literate. Just identify and preserve the means of your status and income. No one holds the public sector accountable.

One of the best models for the African slave experience is that of the Jews under the Nazis. The Germans put 400 thousand people in ghettos suited for 50,000 and provided just enough food for 1/3 of them. By creating shortage, you turn a people against itself. Brothers will turn in sisters for food. People will climb over one another to be on the Jewish police forces which brutalized ghetto inhabitants and arranged selections and roundups for the concentration camps. Black markets form and the ability to act as a unit fails.

The author Primo Levi describes this social deterioration in his book "Survival in Auschwitz";

> " . . . in all countries in which a foreign people have set foot as invaders, an analogous position of rivalry and hatred among the subjected has been brought about; and this, like many other human characteristics, could be experienced in the lager in the light of particularly cruel evidence . . .
>
> . . . One has to fight against the current; to battle every day and every hour against exhaustion, hunger, cold and the resulting inertia; to resist enemies and have no pity for rivals; to sharpen one's wits, build up one's patience, strengthen one's will power. Or else, to throttle all dignity and kill all conscience, to climb down into the arena as a beast against other beasts, to let oneself be guided by those unsuspected, subterranean forces which sustain families and individuals in cruel times . . .
>
> . . . here the struggle to survive is without respite, because everyone is desperately and ferociously alone. If some inmate vacillates, he will find no one to extend a helping hand; on the contrary, someone will knock him aside, because it is in no one's interest that there will be one

more burden dragging himself to work every day; and if someone, by a miracle of savage patience and cunning, finds a new method of avoiding the hardest work, a new art which yields him an ounce of bread, he will be esteemed and respected."

Lillian was married to Morris Devezin but went by her maiden name of Greene and assiduously concealed any reference to the Devezin part of her identity. This was in part to ensure her security and also to hide her connection to the arrest records of sons Morris Jr. and Nelson Devezin, her own divorce proceedings and the fact that her bailiff, Doreasa, was also a Devezin and hired pursuant to a practiced nepotism which prevailed in the county. The County Prosecutor, Bill Mason, arranged county employment for thirteen of his relatives.

Doreasa was responsible for the incomprehensible docket management by which orders were entered prior to required hearings, hearings were scheduled after rulings and in which factual errors were common. It was normal for Defendants to be listed as Plaintiffs and for motions to be assigned to the wrong party. Delays of over six months were common for the simplest activities. Attorneys were often forced to make special trips to her office and beg for rulings on motions filed more than a half-year prior. The Ohio Rules for the Superintendence of Courts require that motions be heard no later than 120 days after they are filed. Most judges get them done in 30 days. Writs of *Procedendo* to the Ohio Supreme Court were necessary to stimulate production in her office. One of her staff attorneys named Stephen Moody recorded her voice mail. He had to pronounce her name twice on the message to get it right. He sounded like Leon Spinks on a bad day. It was no longer necessary to articulate English to work for Judge Lillian.

My acquaintance with Lillian Greene started in 2005, after my father died. My father was a professor of law and advanced management. His credentials included a JD from George Washington University and a PhD in Public Administration. He was a distinguished intellect, author and philosopher. He also was among the first in the country to develop black executives when the stigma against colored people was an active convention. This benevolence runs in my family. My grandfather was a Russian immigrant who took on negro apprentices back when you had your business boycotted and your ass kicked for significant associations with colored people.

We had a comfortable house near the old library in Cleveland Heights, filled with collectibles. After my father's demise in 2000, my mother consigned some of the more valuable things with Wolf's Gallery Inc., the local fine arts auctioneer.

The gallery was founded by Michael Wolf and shortly prior to our consignment, was sold to a consortium including George Bielert and members of the Visconsi family. The Visconsis are institutional builders in the region and one of the most quietly influential people in N. Ohio. The name of the company retained the "Wolf's" association.

Bielert et al. acquired a business they weren't qualified to run and were insolvent at the time they took my mother's consignment. Of course, they didn't publicize their financial circumstances and conducted themselves very discreetly. Their staff of experts came over to catalogue our items. It was quite reassuring and even pleasurable to speak with them. "Wolfs" had specialists in painting, furniture, jewelry and books. The whole thing was civilized and evolved. These people couldn't be part of something deceitful. Their lives were devoted to the non-functional and elevated activities of humans and art. These elegant people wouldn't tolerate the uncertainty of cunning and embezzlement. One would assume that a staff like this represented the healthy financial status of its employer to support it.

Well, we were wrong. "Wolf's" realized $25,000.00 from the sale of my mother's collectibles and gave her nothing. I immediately started research on the company and discovered that it was operating under a variety of similar names such as "Wolf's Gallery Inc.", Wolf's Gallery LLC", "eWolfs.com" and one or two others. The most recent name would replace the immediately prior name which became a defunct business. They were signing their contracts in the name of defunct businesses while assigning assets to the most recent and active business name. Anyone who sued them would be diverted into a dead company. I went over to their place of business. It was deserted. No one would return calls.

As it turned out, Bielert and "Wolf's" were cheating several parties in several states.

I filed suit in Cuyahoga County Court of Common Pleas. I wanted to pierce the corporate veil of the most recent "Wolf's" incarnation and get individual liability against Bielert and his partners. A corporation is a person for legal purposes and when a party sues a corporation, they are normally limited to corporate assets. However, if the officers or other actors of a corporation have engaged in fraud or criminal activity, it is possible to "pierce the corporate veil" and get individual liability against discreet members of the corporation.

I decided on a novel strategy to pierce the corporate veil. It is necessary to distinguish between different types of corporations. "Wolf's" was operating as an LLC, or Limited Liability Corporation. Ohio law up to that point only addressed more conventional "C" corporations, which have stock-holders and are run by boards separate from the stock-holder/investors. Their relations to third parties are heavily legislated and controlled. Internal procedures are also subject to statute and approved bylaws. A "C" corporation cannot act as the "alter-ego" of its officers. Its decision making is indirect and highly regulated.

LLCs, on the other hand, are quite different and were a relatively new creation at the time of my suit. They were originally inflicted on the public by the Wyoming legislature and combined the properties of a partnership and a corporation. The Ohio statute authorized LLCs in 1994.

LLCs allowed investors to act as officers/owners and give them much more fluent and direct control of the company. The LLC is essentially the "alter ego" of the individual members. The LLC statutes tend to be cursory and summarize the internal relations between the members of the LLC, but entirely neglect the relation between the LLC and third parties. The LLC is also protected by the corporate veil. The assets of individual members are protected from suit, despite the fact the company is basically the will and behavior of the individual members who can exercise this will immediately, without the "C" corporation notice to shareholders, informative meetings and a shareholder vote prior to significant activity.

Ohio has one of the most protective standards for piercing the corporate veil. It is very difficult to do and the law covering it contemplates "C" corporations. A new and lower standard needed to be imposed to pierce the veil of an LLC, which did not merit the same protection as a "C" corporation. The individual members of an LLC have direct control of the company. Their decisions have immediate effect and can be made without the formalities, notice and legal restrictions of a "C" corporation. An LLC is a fiction that the company is not an individual proprietorship or partnership. It's a lie designed to reduce the risk of entrepreneurial activity at the expense of accountability to outsiders.

My original filing was assigned to J. Nancy Margaret Russo. Her reputation was terrible. Everyone couldn't say enough bad things about her. It turns out, she was the very best person among those before whom this case was heard. J. Russo dismissed the case on a procedural basis. I appealed to the Eighth District Court of Appeals, and won. J. Russo made it a point to send her clerk to the appellate court to hear the oral arguments. He called later to congratulate me on my presentation. The whole thing seemed so redemptive. I could defend my mom. Judges were capable of self-reflection. Intellectual and moral discipline prevailed.

When an appellate court decides in favor of a party, it remands, or sends the case back to the court of first resort. On the basis of anecdotal information, I had asked J. Russo to remove herself prior to the remand.

She granted the request and that made all the difference.

The case was re-assigned to J. Lillian Devezin Greene. Two years had passed since the original filing. Opposing counsel had still not even answered the Complaint and Default Judgment was in order. A Case Management Conference was scheduled in Ohio. The CMC notice said it was to take place before the judge. I drove in from Vermont and went to the appointed chambers. I was met by the judge's staff attorney; a pretty girl named Tracey Gonzalez.

Case Management Conferences are an opportunity for the judge to meet all parties and get a feel for the characters with whom he/she is dealing. Ostensibly, they are to set a schedule for dispositive motions, discovery, arbitration-alternative dispute resolution and future meetings. They tend to be short, but can give a sense of how the judge feels about a case. Judges can provide innuendo about their preferences and indicate whether the thing is worth a trial or perhaps that a particular party is better off settling . . . quickly. Unless a pleading is defective on its face, judges leave the parties to conduct the case. It is important for a judge to show restraint prior to the conduct of evidence discovery.

I waited for the judge to appear and when it was clear neither the judge nor opposing counsel was going to attend, we started our dialogue. Tracey was styling. She knew she was good looking and in charge of what was perceived to be, (in t he past), a responsible and cerebral enterprise. Every time she spoke, she smiled in appreciation of what she just said. It was like an administrative version of "The Cosby Show" or "Moesha".

"Well, Mr. Grundstein, we feel you should plan on appealing this case."

This was not going well. I started to get scared. An ethically and intellectually unqualified mentality was exercising institutional advantage. What does she mean "appeal"? I just won an appeal. The case is two years old. I want my Mom's money. Only 10% of cases are successful on appeal. My appeal was a significant victory and special certification that the case has merit. We hadn't even done discovery yet. Judges aren't supposed to hold or express bias.

"Ms. Gonzalez, I don't understand, the case has just been remanded to J. Greene. Is she available today?"

"No, I'm presiding over this meeting. You should tell me of your concerns."

"Well, why do you mention "appeal" at this time. A little premature, don't you think?"

"That's just the way we feel about this case, Mr. Grundstein."

"Has anyone heard from opposing counsel?"

"No, but it seems they will not be attending."

"The record shows defendant has not answered my original Complaint. Do you think your judge would hear a motion for Default Judgment, prior to an appeal?"

"Yes Mr. Grundstein. You may file for default judgment. I can't promise anything."

"Ms. Gonzalez, how will we make the Case Schedule? Opposing counsel is not here. How can we agree on a schedule for discovery and dispositive motions?"

" I guess we can't do that at this time. But thank you for coming from Vermont".

Tracey was becoming over-stimulated by the sound of her voice. She could barely conceal her self-exhilaration. In a five minute interval she managed to spoil the legitimate expectations of someone who spent a day and a half to get there. I drove over 700 miles for smarmy posturing and unapologetic misapplication of legal prerogative? Why didn't they just call me and say they were going to give the case to opposing counsel?

I filed for default judgment which was denied without an opinion. There were no findings of fact or law. This was disorienting. If a party hasn't filed an answer after 28 days, default judgment has to be entered. See Ohio Rule of Civil Procedure 55(a):

> "(a) Entering a Default. When a party against whom a judgment for affirmative relief is sought has failed to plead or otherwise defend and that failure is shown by affidavit or otherwise, the clerk must enter the party's default."

Subsequent to that disappointment, I decided to go for content and returned to the original design of my case. My argument to the appellate court was that liability was not limited to the corporate form and that piercing the corporate veil was a right when a corporate member commits a crime or a tort. Maybe the judge was more adapted to legal argument. I'd present her with authority to establish a new standard of veil piercing adapted to LLCs. This would work with a judge who reads her files. A very good attorney in Medina, Ohio was an expert on LLCs. She wrote an article about the need for litigation around LLCs to examine and correct their defects. They posed too many risks to third parties who deal with them. An exegetical process was needed that the legal system could provide. The idea of the legal system is to examine ideas. Democratic theory relies on speech and counter-speech.

J. Lillian refused to rule on my first motion to pierce the corporate veil. There was absolute silence. To be thorough, I made a 2nd brief and motion to supplement my first veil piercing brief and requested a hearing. This time I got a ruling, if you want to call it that. It was a strident Docket rebuke composed by someone instructed to articulate any contrivance to flush this case . . . It said,

"There are no defendants to hold liable".

The tone was more of a declamation than a reasoned opinion. I felt like someone was shouting at me. I made another motion to have the case moved to the "Complex Docket" in the event Lillian's staff couldn't understand it. Another militant Docket entry was made;

"This is not a complex case."

There were defendants. I served them. The appellate court recognized them and insisted they be held accountable. This recognition became the "law of the case", a doctrine which states an issue decided by a court in a case is decisive with respect to that issue and can't be revisited. The appellate court remanded the case to the lower court for litigation against the defendants.

I felt the obstinacy of J. Greene's court and its personalized creation of what it considered to be "law". It reminded me of the loud name calling in which rival children would engage through the athletic field fence in elementary school. Dialogue wasn't the standard. Exchanges were won by shows of will, volume and the disproportionate accumulation of participants on one side or another. If one can martial enough force, a party can avoid dialogue and the scrutiny of intellectual and ethical defects. Just make more noise than the other side. This was a legal system?

I asked around to see what could explain the court's behavior. A veteran attorney said Greene probably gave it to her staff attorney and told her to get rid of it. Greene was always looking for ways to clear her docket. "She's not the hardest working judge." Others were less kind . . . "you wouldn't believe the things she does . . . you wouldn't beLIEVE the things she does" . . . ("we can't take your case").

Opposing counsel never answered any of my briefs. He never bothered to plead or answer, even after the case was active after the appeal. It seemed as if he knew everything would work in his favor. I looked up his credentials. His name was Stephen Dodd and he went to Bob Jones University. Bob Jones is a fundamentalist Christian University, which didn't allow inter-racial dating. Its segregationist policies are well known. It made some adjustment to this policy in the year 2000, after G.W. Bush visited the campus, but Jews were allowed to live in Germany after 1945, too.

In April of 2005, I called Stephen out of curiosity to see if there really was an opposing counsel. He was wholesome, confident and spoke in emotional conclusions which represented decisions about what he thought were the best interests of everyone. It was like being in an old Pat Boone movie. He felt his ability to create consensus and the illusion that he cared about you. Under his supervision and initiative, we could all work towards our common welfare in an environment of Christian conviviality. I asked if he wanted to settle. His client was responsible for a $25,000.00 loss. He offered $3,000.00 which I refused. I expected a trial would cost his client at least $7,000.00. My mom was worth more. I thought I had some leverage. He promised to get back to me.

He did get back to me. The next docket entry was a motion under ORC 2323.52. This is the Ohio Vexatious litigator statute. Dodd wanted to have me declared "vexatious" in Ohio. I looked up the statute and found that Ohio drafted legislation by which it could permanently ban a *pro se* litigant from all Ohio courts, forever, unless that party had permission from the court that imposed filing restrictions, to file. I couldn't believe this sort of legislation could exist in our country. Courts exist for intellectual dialogue. Someone always loses in court. You have the right to be wrong and serial suits without merit can quickly be dismissed by Civil Rule 12 or the application of *res judicata* and collateral *estoppel*. In addition, giving the court that imposed filing restrictions the right to censor all future cases creates the possibility that a court can silence a litigant for an illegal reason, or to prevent that court's bad behavior from being publicized. It's the pimp theory of management. Kill the person you just cheated. Silent people don't bear witness.

This was unchristian. Opposing counsel must respect motherhood and loyalty to one's family. Jesus says so. What's a legal victory without moral content? Surely our wholesome crusader from "Bob Jones University" wouldn't create the possibility of a corrupted procedural victory at the expense of substance. Would White Christendom encourage a court dispensation on the basis of local affiliation and superior knowledge of that court's foibles and marginal ability to read and organize ideas?

At the time this situation had more comic than intellectual value but I became uncertain and re-read the statute. Besides the fact that it uses the term "vexatious" to define what "vexatious" behavior is for purposes of applying the statute, it also required a new action with a new Complaint, Summons and Service. ORC 2323.52 is very clear. It can't be raised by motion. In addition, the statute contemplates serial actions. It doesn't say how many actions, but its badly articulated idea is to restrict people who file "a lot" without legal cause to inconvenience another party.

A little more research led to a history of statutes that impose filing restrictions. These statutes were originally designed to limit "Jail-House" litigants who sought to file scores of actions against parties they felt were responsible for their incarceration or on the basis of alleged prison conditions claimed to be Constitutional violations. Most states don't have them and the federal standard for statutes that impose filing restrictions is articulated in "Cromer v Kraft Foods Inc.", 390 F.3d 812 (2004) (US Ct. App, 4th circuit). "Cromer" says filing restrictions can't be imposed on a permanent basis against all future defendants. It says filing restrictions can only be imposed to protect one, particular defendant in a cause relating to one, particular subject matter or transaction which has already been resolved in court. Ohio's statute allows a judge to permanently ban a litigant from all courts against all potential defendants. The ignorance of this legislation is spectacular, but to be expected in Ohio. You don't exclude someone from their Constitutional right of court access on the basis of a status.

An Ohio appellate court agreed with me and prior to my mother's defense, had declared ORC 2323.52 to be unconstitutional. I called judges Brogan and Shaw who wrote the opinion. They were redemptive and humane. See a portion of their opinion, below:

> "the procedure established by R.C. 2323.52, the vexatious litigator statute, fails to provide a reasonable and meaningful substitute for direct access to Ohio's trial courts. We therefore **determine that the statute is unconstitutional in its entirety as violative of Ohio Const., Art. I Sec. 16 . . .**"

The court continued to say that "no means of review, whether through *mandamus* proceedings or direct appeal, could "remedy the wholly vague and arbitrary nature of the underlying determination." In support, the court reasoned that "the vexatious litigator statute vests complete authority to determine the validity of virtually all of a person's statewide legal actions in one trial court," while leaving unresolved "[e]xactly what constitutes 'an abuse of process' * * * [or] what situations might constitute 'reasonable grounds' for leave to proceed." In addition, the statute does not require "any sort of fact finding process" and "there is no requirement that the trial court articulate upon the record whatever factual or legal grounds may have been the basis for its decision to deny leave to proceed." Accordingly, the court concluded, leave could be arbitrarily and summarily denied "upon a formally proper complaint that would ordinarily survive a motion to dismiss under Civ.R. 12(B)(6)." ("Mayer v. Bristow" 1999 Ohio App.933, and cited in "Ohio Transit Authority v Timson" 132 Ohio App.3d at 53)

A beautiful statement; evolved and independent minds articulating a standard which has universal application.

Just the kind which would offend the Ohio Supreme Court which immediately reversed. Chief Justice Alice Resnick-Robie wrote the order to reinstate ORC 2323.52. Her opinion is a narcissistic, intellectual failure based on serial cliches and platitudes. She cited the need to keep bad cases off the docket but provided no statistical or fact basis for the burden placed on Courts by *pro se* litigators. The Rand Corporation actually did a study on this subject and found that individual litigators are disposed of quite efficiently (in less than an hour of a judge's time) through Civil Rules 8 and 12 by which a case is dismissed if it has no basis in law, fact or jurisdiction. This same study said the real burden on courts comes from the large firm tort actions which can take years to resolve and need rooms of archive space to store the discovery materials. But no one holds large firms accountable. They have too many resources, staff, contribute to elections, support the State Bar and are so financially exhilarating.

Robie's opinion is a "How to Fail a Legal Analysis Test", for 1st year law students. It also failed to recognize definitional characteristics of the procedures she cited as authority in her favor. Alice was subsequently arrested for Driving While Intoxicated by the Ohio State Police and during the stop asked the police to let her slide because, "I give you guys good rulings all the time".

Resnick-Robie said *pro se* litigants didn't have to worry about arbitrary denials of "leave to proceed" because if a court refused permission to file, a party could just file for a Writ of *Mandamus*. This sort of ignorance should not be published. If I was that stupid I would never argue. Writs of *Mandamus* have original jurisdiction in the state appellate courts. The Ohio Vexatious Litigator statute restricts a party from filing in the state appellate court without "leave to proceed". Access to the courts is still contingent. One can't file for a writ of *Mandamus* without permission. Writs of *Mandamus* are also available from the State Supreme Court, but they aren't granted to "vexatious" parties. I tried several times. There is a de facto exclusion of *pro se* filers who were declared "vexatious".

Secondly, Writs of *Mandamus* are to compel a government agency to perform a non-discretionary act. The most famous example in American legal literature is the Writ of *Mandamus* in the case of "Marbury v. Madison". Outgoing Secretary of State John Marshall signed a commission to Marbury designating him as a Justice of the Peace. The new Secretary of State, James Madison, wouldn't give it to him and Marbury sued for the piece of paper proving his status. If a Secretary of State signed the commission, it had to be delivered. (Yes, even our mythologized founders engaged in spiteful pissing contests.)

This is quite different from the decision a judge would make about granting "leave to proceed", which is a discretionary act based on a judge's judgment (without the benefit of objective and legal criteria). The decision to grant "leave to proceed", or not, is not subject to *mandamus* because "leave to proceed" is a discretionary act. *Mandamus* does not apply to discretionary acts. How could the other justices sign this opinion? These people can't be trusted with a legal system.

So, Resnick-Robie does a lot of damage, gets stopped drunk by the State Police and staggers off with a generous pension; a distinguished career making the legal system significantly worse on an institutional basis, without accountability.

I drafted a response to the motion and filed it within the prescribed time of 30 days. I described the procedural requirements of ORC 2323.52 to the court and pointed out the jurisdictional defects of the motion. The statute required a new action with a new Complaint, Summons and Service. It's an easy jurisdictional analysis. Without a new action, the court has no power to act. Jurisdiction does not attach.

Jurisdiction is an idea, or accumulation of several ideas, on which all attorneys and courts rely every day, but which is incompletely understood and under-examined. It has three forms, all of which must be met for a court to hear a case. Without jurisdiction, anything a court does is void from the start and without enforceability. Jurisdictional arguments are among the first things examined in a case, because without jurisdiction, a court cannot proceed.

The first part of jurisdiction is Territorial. A court can only hear cases based on law applicable within its territory and for events which happened there. Unless there is a sufficient fact nexus to a piece of land, there is no Territorial Jurisdiction on which a court can act. For instance, if someone steals a car in Kentucky and remains in Kentucky, a party can't sue in Ohio.

Territorial Jurisdiction is also an expression of comity and Republican Government, which allows states to determine the culture of law within their own state. States are still bound by the Constitution, but federal courts will give a presumption of legitimacy to a state determination of law which is challenged in federal court. Comity gives states the right to diverge from one another, while the Constitution and Federal Courts limit the extent of divergence. All the states have to have a common Constitutional intent.

Comity extends beyond interstate applications. Ohio has a very strong "Home Rule" doctrine in their constitution, so there can be significant variation between municipalities and counties in Ohio on Constitutional issues. This was particularly evident with hand-gun control laws at the turn of the 21st century. Every suburb of Cleveland had different gun laws and it was possible to drive across 3-4 towns and switch from being compliant to non-compliant at each border. A 2nd amendment analysis of Ohio gun law in the year 2000 would have kept an attorney busy for a year. But the point is simple, court jurisdiction is geographically limited to events within described borders.

The second part of jurisdiction is Subject Matter Jurisdiction. Subject Matter Jurisdiction describes the content a court can scrutinize. For example, some courts only have criminal misdemeanor jurisdiction and can't hear felonies. Some courts can only hear civil claims for amounts less than a certain dollar amount; (Small claims, municipal courts). Some courts can only hear contract claims; (a limitation common to Small Claims courts) Some courts have concurrent jurisdiction for all amounts and can hear all civil and criminal claims. What is less understood about Subject Matter Jurisdiction is that it doesn't attach, or find application, until there is compliance with Territorial and *In Personam Jurisdiction*. Subject Matter Jurisdiction has to "attach" in order to be active.

In Personam Jurisdiction is the means by which a person is given notice that he is subject to legal action. It must occur for Subject Matter Jurisdiction to attach. 5th Amendment Due Process is "Notice and Hearing". You get told in advance that you have to attend a hearing. It happens when people are "served" with notice of suit. Notice of suit is controlled by statute. It can happen when someone runs up to you and gives you a summons or when the police serve a warrant for your arrest. More and more states are allowing service by mail.

So, the means by which subject matter and Territorial Jurisdiction is activated for ORC 2323.52 is when a Complaint and filing fee is sent to the Clerk of Courts. This filing is completed when the complaint is served on a party in compliance with Rule of Civil Procedure 4.

There is a further refinement which needs to be addressed. I was living in Vermont at the time I filed on behalf of my mother. How do you serve a party who has done something in Ohio, but lives in another state? That is covered in the Ohio state Long Arm Statute 2307.381 et seq.. Long arm service is controlled by statute. Every state has one and there must be compliance. Statutes are written because the legislature feels the matter is too important to tolerate the variations which could occur if courts were left to decide a particular matter. In this instance a statute defines if sufficient notice was given to an out-of-state defendant. An action under ORC 2323.52 cannot be commenced against a foreign (other state) party, without long arm compliance. Anything that happens in court absent service has no legal existence or enforceability. I was never served in Ohio or Vermont.

I pointed this out to the court in my brief. There was no Reply by opposing counsel. I waited a couple months assuming that the court would deny the original motion to impose filing restrictions and issue a rebuke against Dodd.

Two months later, I received a call from a friend in Ohio.

"Hey, you've just been placed on the Ohio Supreme Court List of Vexatious Litigators".

A feeling of rot accelerated through my corpus. I ran to a computer. There it was. On July 25th, 2005, the Independent New Democratic Republic of Lillian Greene's Office, granted defense motion, without hearing, to have me declared vexatious and subject to filing restrictions for the rest of my life. I could never file anything again without Lillian Devezin-Greene's permission. This was a legal death sentence. Anyone declared vexatious loses all credibility and you are essentially denied legal protection on a *de facto* basis. I became apoplectic with anger and smashed myself against the back of my chair. The drama of unfairness which was part of underclass daily life had found practice in the legal system. The exact thing against which the law protects was now legitimate in the septic ferment of Greene's office. The culture of jurisprudence had been supplemented by the pragmatic mentality of poverty and violence. Written law is ultimately evidence of a culture of thought. Ours was diminishing on a generational basis.

I immediately filed a motion to reconsider and insisted on compliance with the statutory requirements of ORC 2323.52, prior to sanctions. My right of access to court is a property right which couldn't be extinguished or altered without Due Process "notice and hearing". Under the statute, I get a lot more than notice and hearing. A new Complaint has to be filed and served in Vermont. I mean, who are these people? Wasn't their whole posture during the civil rights movement that they were denied legal rights on the arbitrary status of race? Wasn't one of the core (and legitimate) complaints that the legal system became meaningless for them and that they were convicted because of the way they looked? Didn't my peers and classmates march and demonstrate in several cities to make sure these people could enforce their legal rights?

My notions of good-will and social responsibility were betrayed. I was dealing with a distorted and narcissistic ethos that prioritized self-interest at the expense of obligation. Greene-Devezin couldn't be inconvenienced by the law. She needed to maintain an office and to do so entailed diminishing her work-load by excluding litigants who didn't represent personal loss to her or advancement. Dodd worked for a very prosperous and influential law-firm. Devezin-Greene would have to see him and his associates during the course of her career and didn't want to alienate an entity that could hurt her reputation with the Bar Association or jeopardize campaign contributions for her next election. I saw this time and again in Cleveland during subsequent actions. Judges would give attorneys they knew anything that attorney wanted, even if it entailed violation of the clearest statutory provisions.

Lillian ordered a hearing AFTER her order. It was shameless. If I was that stupid I wouldn't post on public dockets. Normally, the hearing comes first. I moved to strike the hearing because there was no jurisdiction for any determinations under ORC 2323.52 in the first place. Dodd asked for attorney fees and sanctions.

Lillian awarded him $10,000.00. She wrote an opinion in which she found I called opposing counsel a name and said, "This court will not begin to address the legal or procedural deficiencies of Plaintiff's case" . . . Gee, I didn't mean to inconvenience Lillian with thought and analysis. That's her job. There is no basis for *any* ruling without an analysis of legal and procedural issues. Lillian used the presumption of competence and scholarship attached to her office to exercise a failed administration of lazy homilies and judgment unreferenced to any legal standards. The last have become first. The unclean administer the clean. Those oppressed by racial discrimination support the attorneys who were educated at racist institutions against those who fought unfair behavior for three generations. A complete undoing. I'd had brighter pets than Lillian Greene.

This was the Bishop Berkeley practice of legal administration. If no one can see the violent offenses practiced by a judge against a litigant, they don't exist. I was fined by the person who stole from my mother and permanently excluded from the legal system for defending an 87 year old widow, psychotic with grief. Lillian proved she was better adapted working as a tunnel support in a construction project than as someone who exercises judgment in support of the social contract.

4

Appeal, Celebrezzes and Plagiarized Papers

"When it comes to the public sector, stupid is better". Prof. N.D. Grundstein

This will be easy. Any imbecile could see that the ruling against me was an anomalous result of a court administration that must hold its meetings and consultations in tunnels and under bridges. This would tweak the conscience of any reasonable Mongol Horde. Besides, Appellate courts operate at a high level. They're paid to correct the defects of lower courts. They can afford to do the right thing.

Ohio Appellate rules 3 and 4 control filing. An appeal of right must be filed within 30 days. Filing deadlines are strictly applied. The order by which I was declared "vexatious" was entered on July 25, 2005. I filed my Notice of Appeal and filing fee on August 15, 2005. A scheduling order was mailed from the 8th District Court of Appeals. It gives deadlines for the submission of written arguments and briefs. My brief was sent on time. A Justice Blackmon sent it back because it wasn't double spaced. I corrected the spacing and returned it. Opposing counsel didn't file a brief.

I received a correspondence from the court scheduling oral argument for March of 2006. It was signed by a woman with the unlikely name of Ute Vilfroy. I looked on the court docket to confirm the date. ALL court activity is listed on public and permanent dockets. This includes scheduling orders and administrative correspondence. There was no reference to the Oral Argument or the scheduling letter. I assumed someone made a mistake or it would be added later.

March is the worst time to drive west from Vermont. Since I'm in the North, I have to cross the Green Mountains and Lake Champlain into New York and the Adirondacks. That's two mountain ranges. Domesticated mountains, but still prone to snow and frozen patches. March is also the season for ice storms when rain that seems to be liquid leaves a coating of ice when it lands. Cars become ice bound and trees collapse. It's impossible to walk outside. Driving is unthinkable.

In warm weather it's an interesting drive across distinct American regions. Vermont is the only landlocked New England state and the isolation has allowed it to retain a state character. Vermont was actually an independent Republic for 9 years and never tolerated slavery. It was originally called "New Connecticut" and became the 14th state of the Union. The underground railroad went through Vermont. There is a house with a hidden room in my town of Eden Mills. It was designed to hide slaves until they could finish the last 20 miles into Canada. The abandonment of Primogeniture was also a part of Vermont's state constitution. Sons came from other regions for land which was only available to their oldest brother at home.

The drive takes you through Vermont regions which still rely on forest and agricultural products for their economy, across Lake Champlain and into NY. If you take the southern NY route you go through Rip Van Winkle country which is populated by Gothic homes and where the distinction between English and Dutch names is still mentioned. The Hudson River is also the regional site for the books of Richard Russo, who wrote "Mohawk", "Empire Falls" and "The Risk Pool".

The Adirondacks descend into Utica and the lakes of Central New York. The final portion of the trip brings you north of the Allegheny Mountains to the region known as "The West" in 1820. NE Ohio also belonged to Connecticut and was called its "Western Reserve". The domesticated farmland of Eastern Ohio is the beginning of The Great Plains which actually start a little West of Cleveland Hts., Ohio and end in Colorado. The Amish of Ohio are the first hint of the Germanic and Scandinavian strain that populates the region from Indiana to Minnesota, the Dakotas and south to Texas. There's a reason the capitol of N. Dakota is named "Bismarck".

Vermont displays another significant virtue I have to mention. It rotates its judges from jurisdiction to jurisdiction every year or two. It is a brilliant procedure and prevents judges from forming partisan relations with local attorneys, prosecutors, police, city administrators/politicians and everyone else. It works. The judiciary of Vermont is one of the least criticized in the country.

My trip was grey and uneventful. I arrived at the Old Courthouse in Cleveland which was conceived during the time of Cleveland's ascendance. Cleveland's beacon is actually 1920 when it was a world class industrial city populated by Standard Oil and the Rockefellers, Carnegies, Mathers and the Hannahs. Western Reserve University was the Harvard of the midwest and the Anglo-Celtic people who owned the city sent their children there.

The courthouse is like a cathedral with an empty, 4 story central area where the pews, nave and organ would have been placed. Courtrooms and administrative offices surround the indulgently unused part of the interior in tiered balconies around the perimeter of the open area. Everything about it was entertaining. Even the narrow and tall wooden entrances to administrative offices and the old fashioned painted lettering which identified them.

I entered the ante-room for the court where the hearing was to be held. It was study-like and paneled in dark hardwood. It was an anachronistic class expression of law and public service from a time when these things were believed to be distinguished and learned. The courtroom was paneled in a similar fashion and had 25 foot caisson ceilings which were also carved. Surely something good would happen here.

I took a seat and was approached by a bailiff. Three hearings were scheduled for the morning and I was the first. I don't know how the bailiff knew who I was, but he bent over and whispered, "Your hearing has been re-set to third. You will be the last hearing this morning".

I thought nothing of it. Opposing counsel, S. Dodd, sat three rows in front of me with an adolescent too old to be his son. I assumed it was the son of his client who stole from my mother. They exchanged cliches and reassuring statements about the future of this case. Jesus will provide against the anti-Christ. Dodd was built like a Tight End or Wide Receiver for a small, division 3 college; tall, sturdy and oddly paternal. We passed malevolent looks.

The judges walked in and we all rose. I was sure there must be some mistake. The panel of judges included someone named Frank Celebrezze.

The Celebrezzes have been part of Ohio politics for decades. There's even an Anthony O. Celebrezze building in Cleveland. It's easy to be confused by the Celebrezzes. There are a lot of them in public life and their names repeat. There are 2 Frank Celebrezze Jrs. One Frank Celebrezze Jr., preceded my classmate by a generation and was elected Chief Justice of the Ohio Supreme Court in 1978. He held that office until 1986 when he lost to Thomas Moyer, who accused him of being connected to organized crime. Frank Jr. sued the local newspaper called "The Plain Dealer" when it agreed with Justice Moyer.

Other Celebrezzes include James, who served on the Ohio Supreme Court, Anthony, who was in the Kennedy administration, Anthony J. who was a candidate for Ohio governor and Frank D. (the first) who served as a state judge.

Frank Jr. was in my law school class and could have been described as the least intelligent person in the student body. Since this was Cleveland, he was subject to attack by his peers. The odd thing was his absence of malice. He was very good-natured and never bore a grudge. He always assumed people could reengage after an episode of organized insults conducted at his expense and never maintained an injured or hurt condition.

If his ancestors were not Ohio Supreme Court justices and politicians, Frank would have spent his life driving a bread truck. Frank was a source of endless entertainment and stories composed at his expense. His affable persona projected a diminished and uncertain intellectual capacity. Prior to our law school Property exam, Frank was challenged to define Real Property. One protagonist was a strikingly handsome student of Sicilian descent. He was a confusing combination of possessive friendship and real violence.

"Frank, you're so fucking stupid, you don't even know what Real Property is."

His response was . . . "well, you know . . . land . . . chattels . . . " ("chattels" is the old English word for "cattle" and means Personal Property. It distinguishes moveable property which is "Personal" from immoveable property, which is "Real").

"No dunce. Chattel MEANS personal property. I'm going to smash your head on the pavement just to show you how it feels."

Frank set his mouth to show small and narrow teeth. He intended to project menace and retribution, but he wasn't overtly violent. I always felt compassion for him. He started to become known as "little teeth".

Frank should have been undone when he got caught cheating on his first year writing project.

Cleveland Marshall College of Law was populated by Clevelanders, many of whom were the first generation in their family to graduate from college. The generation of Frank's parents was born and/or raised during the depression. Poverty and class discrimination was an active part of living memory for that time. There was a large contingent of Irish and Italian Catholics and a small sample of residents who went to undergraduate colleges in other states, but who returned to Ohio for the reduced tuition rates of a state school. Law school was a revelation in work for many of the students. The classwork and assignments occupied all the time between 7:30 a.m. and midnight. Over 30% of those who entered didn't finish.

The first year writing project was part of a mandatory Legal Writing program. Everyone had to take Legal Writing. The course was in two parts and lasted a school year. The culmination of the course was the production of a very long and researched paper which was to reflect the skills and techniques taught during the year. Course work began in September. The paper was due the following year at the end of April. It was wise to have started the paper by January.

Legal writing was divided into small sections with 10-15 students per instructor. It was impossible to be anonymous.

Professor Klein taught the section which included Frank Celebrezze. One of the students in Frank's section was a particularly disciplined person from Buffalo, NY and had completed his paper a month before it was due. Frank asked the Buffalo student if he could use his paper to help with formatting his own. Frank was apparently having trouble deciding how to organize his arguments. The Buffalo student agreed and lent Frank his paper for a week. Frank returned it and two weeks later, everyone in Ms. Klein's section turned in their papers.

A week after submission, Ms. Klein dismissed the class as usual but insisted that Frank and the Buffalo student remain after class. She locked the door.

Ms. Klein received two identical papers. They had the same number of pages, paragraphs, language and format. The only essential difference was the signature. Frank had plagiarized the Buffalo student's paper. Not only was this dishonest, but shows a failure of judgment at the sub-cretin level. Did he think the teacher would lose track of 12 papers? Did he think the teacher wouldn't remember two identical papers? In addition, what sort of person inflicts this kind of risk on someone who was willing to help? What about your family reputation? Frank seemed indifferent to the fact that his generational presence could end the Celebrezze name as an acceptable candidate for public office. Everyone waited for a loud noise.

Nothing happened to Frank.

In Cleveland, being dishonest is a criterion for participation in public life. Stupid is better, too. In a politicized system, income and position are the prevailing values. The Political Science 101 definition of politics is "competition for resources under conditions of scarcity". It says nothing about being skilled, honest, intellectually able or noble. It's a fight for stuff.

The values of maintenance, income and control have priority over Constitutional jurisprudence. Public systems such as Cleveland function on the basis of race, religion, ethnicity and Labor Union Affiliation. Car bombings were common during the '70s. A professor at Cleveland State had his car attacked in the 80s. It contained evidence for use in a Union trial. The paramount skill in a corrupt administration is the ability to maintain the group that provides your income. People you can't see run things.

Professor Klein would not pander to a family name and reported the plagiarism to the dean. The dean of the law school was a man named Bogomolny. Frank could be seen walking to and from the Dean's office during class hours, but he was not suspended or expelled. There was no publicity about the event in the law school newspaper. The dean did not address the matter. The local newspaper didn't pick it up. A year later, a local judge called for a legal assistant and specifically asked for Frank, who adopted a brief case for his new status.

The year Frank took the Ohio Bar is alleged to have the highest pass rate . . . Ever. Everybody was said to have passed.

Since I was re-scheduled to last, the courtroom was empty. All the other litigants and their attorneys who preceded me left and only 3 people in the seating remained; me, opposing counsel and his adolescent companion. A sturdy bald man presided. His name was Corrigan and he was not on the list of judges to preside over this hearing. Why did the Eighth District need a pro tem judge? They had plenty of judges and could even do the oral arguments as a 3 judge panel. I remember the banc clearly, it included Frank Celebrezze, Diane Karpinski, Patricia Blackmon, Collen Cooney and a woman who projected contempt named Anne Dyke.

I was called to the lectern. Corrigan spoke energetically and without remorse:

"Mr. Grundstein, oral arguments have been canceled and the appeal is dismissed."

I wasn't ready for this. I just drove 750 miles at the instruction of this court. This must be the reason they had a pro tem judge. He could do their dirty work without a permanent connection to the court.

"Your honor, I was instructed to come here by the court administrator's office. I have the correspondence. This court cannot contradict those instructions. It is estopped to do so. In addition, Ohio Rules of Appellate Procedure 3 and 4 control this action and I have complied with them. This court accepted my filing fee and brief."

The judge replied; "The court has determined that you are "vexatious" and will not allow you to proceed with this appeal."

"Surely I get a first right of appeal to challenge a lower court order entered without jurisdiction. An appellate rule is a state law. It has to be followed. In addition, the equitable notion of *estoppel* would prevent this court from striking the appeal and this hearing. *Estoppel* says a party cannot contradict itself if a second party has relied on the representations of the first party and acted on those representations. I just drove a long way. And, what about Ohio Constitution, Article 1, Section 16; § 1.16 "Redress in courts" (1851, amended 1912):

> "All courts shall be open, and every person, for an injury done him in his land, goods, person, or reputation, shall have remedy by due course of law, and shall have justice administered without denial or delay."

I abandoned the formality of the exchange.

"What about my mom? I'm vindicating the rights of my widowed mother.

She was 87 years old and just lost my father. Doesn't that count? We have to protect the most vulnerable among us."

"Mr. Grundstein., the court has decided. Case dismissed."

There was no apology, explanation or attempt to acknowledge the Ohio Constitution and the destruction of my legitimate expectations. I didn't understand the lack of conscience, but was learning that the human mind adapts ideas to what it needs them to mean. The idea of conscience can be warped and will apply moral value to self-interest. Morality becomes the equivalent of self-interest.

If a court feels it has to destroy the rights of a party to maintain its partisan relations and personal agendas, it will assign moral value to its ethical failures because its ethical failures support the group and its participating individuals. One's greatest obligation is to oneself and an individual in Cleveland public life can't serve himself without group affiliation. Never mind that a judge is paid and sworn to uphold the law and a culture of fairness. In addition, consciences tend not to become active until there is a public consensus to expose and punish bad deeds. It's not so bad if no one knows. I was among people who couldn't afford to manage the ethical design of American law. The Cleveland judicial administration prioritized the agenda of some meat-ball Judge in Common Pleas over a family that really trusted and contributed to the quality of public life in Cleveland.

Dodd gave me a self-confirmed look of victory. He was part of an operating consensus and could extract moral confirmation from corrupt acts. It didn't matter how good my arguments were or how wrong the court was, I was excluded from the group of people who controlled the legal system. Jurisprudence didn't matter. Being white didn't matter. Maybe being Irish Catholic would have helped. Speculation didn't help.

I ran up to the office where the staff attorneys worked and asked to speak with one of them. A man named Dave Parchem came out and said he couldn't explain the behavior of the judges. He had no influence on what he referred to as "command decisions". The list of staff attorneys included someone named John G. Cooney. He is the husband of Judge Colleen Cooney, before whom I just appeared fifteen minutes prior. I imagined the conversations between them. "John, we have a situation with the lower court. Give us a means to hide this case."

What Record?

Normally, all hearings in all state courts are recorded. I ordered a recording of the hearing. None was made. There was no record of the hearing. I also checked the docket to confirm the hearing date for oral argument assigned on the letter from court administrator Ute Vilfroy. There was no docket entry. There was no public record that oral argument was to be held. There was no public record that this hearing or set of events occurred. The only recorded docket entry subsequent to this March meeting was one which said "case dismissed".

I'd just entered the perimeter of a county legal system which exempted itself from the ethical and Constitutional culture of the US. Or maybe, it just represented the most recent expression of that culture.

I was now de facto excluded from all Ohio courts. The courts paid to protect my rights made sure I didn't have them. What about my mom?

5

Arraignment and More Charges;
Employment for Sex in Bedford Municipal Court

"You must tour our jails"

The Vermont arrest and proceedings of October, 2007 forced me to Ohio. I drove all night to attend the arraignment in Cuyahoga County Court of Common Pleas. It was just before Christmas, 2007. The Justice Center is a 31 story monolith. It was built in 1976 and is slightly stained from use and drifting detritus in the atmosphere. I joined the thick procession of primarily African-American defendants organizing themselves into a single file at the security check. We emptied our pockets and put cases on the conveyor to be x-rayed. Arrivals then moved past the large police counter and east to the banks of elevators. Columns of air were pushed and pulled like a strange kind of mechanical respiration as the elevator went up and down and their doors opened and closed for the next cycle of movement. The demographics of the justice system could be seen in the elevators. The attorneys were primarily white and well-dressed. Defendants were primarily black and in casual wear. Police were over-sized and in uniform. Many of the defendants wore things I'm sure they felt were special, but were really adapted to an informal birthday party or date.

It was always safer to go up in an elevator first thing in the morning than to go down in one later after the first sets of hearings. I've had to escape from elevators when I became the arbitrary object of class and race resentment after a bad day in court.

I checked in at the arraignment desk as instructed. It was wedged against a wall in a hallway between the courtrooms on that floor. A contingent of primarily black people sat in the banks of chairs in a waiting area. After a short wait, we were all called into a large courtroom and took a seat wherever we wanted.

Arraignments are short proceedings in which charges are read against a party and he has an opportunity to plead guilty, not guilty or *no lo contendere*. Not much takes place at them and affirmative defenses are not presented. In addition to the plea, the only thing of real consequence is the amount of bail to be set. This can determine whether a party remains free or incarcerated until his trial. A T.V. screen flickered above the judge's bench. This was to arraign parties who were in jail. Some parties are incarcerated prior to arraignment because they have been determined to be dangerous and/or significant flight risks.

J. John Russo was presiding and made it a point to make this a light event. He was a young 40 and bounced in his seat while making promises about how he was going to bring bagels and cream cheese to the next sitting on Friday. He was polite to everyone and solicitous of the defendants. After a bail determination, he'd ask if the defendant thought it was fair. "Is that O.K.? Is that fair?" I don't know if they could determine or control what was fair during their arraignment, but J. Russo didn't want to diminish or scare people needlessly. Most of the accused didn't have attorneys and represented themselves. Many were accompanied by family members. Subdued dialogues of the accused consulting with their friends, family and attorneys took place while the judge spoke to a particular defendant.

I had no experience with this and when my turn came, I stood, approached the bench and plead "Not Guilty". My bail was "personal recognizance" as promised. I was asked to sit down again and wait. Why couldn't I leave?

I waited for a bit and turned to a taciturn boy who couldn't have been more than 17. He was reluctant to speak and looked quietly offended that I addressed him. "White" meant "suspicious".

"What's next?', I asked.

"You never did this before?".

"No. Why can't I just leave? Bail's set."

"Man, we have to go back to a holding cell while they check for warrants."

I didn't know about this. After about 15 minutes of watching men and women in orange suits get arraigned from jail, I was led to a door on the side of the courtroom. It opened into a narrow corridor with 3 long cells on each side. Women and men were separated. We kept all our personal property and clothing. I remained in my suit jacket and tie. There was no place to put my legal folders and briefs, so I just held them. There were about 15 people in my cell and we had teenagers and middle-aged men. Everyone was polite. There were no aggressive displays between us. One particularly robust boy who made his living trash picking in Cleveland felt it was necessary to challenge the guard. He resisted instructions and started shouting at the jailer, who was also black and about 250 lbs. When the guard asked him to be quiet, the boy became more aggressive and started challenging the guard.

"Go on . . . smack me. Go on . . . hit me. You think you tell me what to do? I'll smack you when I get out of here."

The guard, whose manner was world weary prior to this prisoner display, lost his temper and started shouting back and forth with the boy. Eventually, he entered our cell with another guard and took him out. We all compressed to the rear of the holding tank to make room for the additional over-sized bodies and a fight. It looked like a stressful job. It can't be easy to see your people enter jail by the gross, every day, and have to contain them too.

There was very little room and sitting was almost impossible without bumping someone else. I assumed this was a strategy to punish us or turn us against one another, but there was surprisingly little tension in the room. Everyone made it a point to get along and speak politely. I was squatting next to a caramel colored adolescent with the name "Andre" tattooed across his neck. He was an vivid mix of negro and Caucasian with generous lips and a shell-like nose. I assumed this was an incendiary combination in his neighborhood and expected the worst when he shifted and I tipped into him.

"My bad" he said. "You all right?"

I was completely disarmed; relieved too. The small faced boy with whom I spoke in the courtroom was with us and we all started to talk and share our experiences. One undersized white person with a dreary mustache made exasperated facial gestures and said he was in for "some kind of bullshit accounting fraud". Most of the kids were in for drugs. Two garrulous white guys were in for receiving stolen property. Everyone looked at me for my story. I didn't know what to say. I couldn't claim I didn't do anything and that I was the object of a judge-police-prosecutor conspiracy. So I just told them I threatened a judge in court. Everyone nodded and seemed satisfied. It sounded reasonable and certainly within everyone's range of experience. Who wouldn't want to threaten a judge? When they asked about the folders, my tie and jacket, I told them I was an attorney. That added to my popularity. We all started talking about arrests and I listened to stories of people with long criminal histories. It became a chatty and happy cell.

People were removed one by one as warrant checks were completed. Our little party was being terminated by subtraction. I watched my new friends leave and could extend my legs as more room was made. Finally, my name was called. I was one of the last. A huge guard addressed me;

"Goldberg", he said, looking at me over his clipboard.

"Sir, that's Grundstein", I corrected.

"That's what I said, Greenberg." He moved his head from side to side and frowned at me. It wasn't hostile. He was just having a little fun. We both knew it. It was funny and drained the tension of the day.

"Grundstein".

"O.K. Mr. Goldman, we have a warrant on you."

"What do you mean? How is that possible? I just turned myself in from Vermont on a warrant from Cleveland."

"Tough break. Got another one. Something from Chagrin Falls. Load o' White People there. They don't like either of us in that neighborhood. Right Steinberg? We're moving you there. They'll pick you up with their own police. In the meantime, let's go down the hall."

I was led to another cell two doors down the corridor, towards the courtroom. I was in it alone. The guard didn't lock the door.

"You just stay here Steinberg. Don't go anywhere. I'm not going to lock the door."

"That's Grundstein".

"That's what I said, Goldstein. You'll be fine. Just don't be acting like that bad boy before. You know, that boy who wanted to fight me."

"He had a very developed death wish."

"Crazy people all over. Jail does it to some. Now you just stay here Feldman."

I sat in the cell alone. After 20 minutes, I was led to an elevator and lowered to a much larger holding cell off a police parking area. We passed a queue of prisoners in orange suits being led somewhere. One boy whispered something venomous to the person in front of him which caused him to turn and square to fight. A large guard ran to separate them. Electric doors buzzed and popped as we passed through the two doors to the new cell. Its population was an older age range. They were bigger, raw and edgier. Someone used the exposed toilet while a muscular black man spread himself out on the fixed table and started talking about the Christian rap music he was going to compose. I didn't want to ask how Christian virtues landed him here. These were people from origins and environments that failed them and set them loose.

An unlikely albino guard with oversized nostrils and huge forearms came in to address us. He wasn't cruel and wanted us to know he would answer any questions we had about transfers.

"I'm not in the habit of lying, so I'm only going to tell you the truth and won't say what I don't know".

We had to be patient while we were either being re-assigned or transferred elsewhere. He didn't know how long things would take because they were waiting on paper work and police from different jurisdictions. He showed empathy for the group. It seemed as if he knew exactly how his people came to be here and didn't want to be self-righteous or act superior. It was a grim comfort. This group seemed to believe nothing good would come of their circumstance. I was one of only two white people in the cell and we didn't mix comfortably. There wasn't the innocence of my prior tank.

My name was called after an hour. I wished everyone well and was led to a waiting patrol car in the underground parking lot where I was passed to an entirely different demographic of police. Two officers from the Chagrin Falls police department took custody. One was an older cop with an anachronistic tough-white guy persona. He cinched me up in a wide leather belt with cuffs while the younger policeman watched. It looked like he was assigned to teach the rookie. The rookie seemed like the type of kid who preferred candy to dating as an adolescent. He was the benignly subnormal boy who sat in the back of class during high school and was given "C"s because although he didn't understand the course material, was passive. I was put in the back seat. The bunker door opened and we drove out of the parking area.

Our route took us through a worn downtown Cleveland and onto the freeway past smokestack industries. We got off the highway on the far east side of Cleveland and drove another 4 miles through increasingly affluent suburbs. The new construction was hard to identify and some of the shopping malls had facades that looked like they were designed by Venetian architects on benzedrine.

The nouveau Italianate quality of the buildings stopped abruptly when we entered Chagrin Falls, which looked like a prosperous, 19th century Vermont town. The houses included late Victorian, mid-19th century revival and cozy bungalow styles. Every home was an appealing and distinct morsel. Its charm and warmth were maintained by a white executive class which extended into the neighboring towns of Hunting Valley and Bainbridge.

New Charges
Fraud is Good in Bedford

I was booked into the cutest jail yet. If you are ever incarcerated for a short time, make sure you schedule something in Chagrin Falls. I owned a condo in the town, and one of the presiding officers recognized me from the times he saw me jogging in the neighborhood. I was brought coffee and hard candies. It was delightful. I was shown a paper with the charges against me and allowed to call a bail-bondsman. The charges recited a portion of the Ohio Revised Code known as "Telephonic Harassment" and a more general charge of "Menacing". The document also contained the fact basis for the charges and referred to a telephone call I made to the finance manager of a condominium I owned in Chagrin Falls. The detective was Tim Reed of the Chagrin Falls police.

The call was made from Vermont several months earlier when I discovered the condominium management had charged all the residents $150,000.00 for a roof that only cost $76,500.00. I called every roofer in the area to find out who did the work and discovered it was done by "Seasons Roofing". I called to confirm the discrepancy between the amount assessed against the residents and the bill given to the condominium management. The owner of "Seasons" was honorable and sent me the invoice. He had nothing to hide. Our condo did. The condo had a reputation for financial misdeeds and dishonesty. The manager, a man named Fred Agresta, was referred to by local realtors as "The Most Hated Man in Chagrin Falls".

When I discovered the fraud on the condominium ownership, I lost my temper and left a message with the finance director, a woman named Debbie Kuhn. The call originated in Vermont. The message was:

"I'm sick of your criminal behavior. Get the fuck out of my condominium or I'll smear you across the parking lot."

In response, the manager ran to the local police and filed a complaint. The police detective spoke with the Bedford prosecutor, Tom Hanculak, and a complaint was filed. A warrant for my arrest was also issued which included a bail requirement. I couldn't get out of jail until I paid. It was odd. Cuyahoga County indicted me for a second degree felony and let me go without bond. Chagrin Falls insisted on two bonds of $1500.00 for charges that were misdemeanors and which should be dismissed without trial in a decent system.

The discrepancy between the roofer bill and the condominium assessment was the reason I sued the condominium earlier in the year before Judge Junkin of the local court. As the reader will remember, Junkin dismissed the case at the preliminary stages without hearing evidence or any other analysis of facts and law. I was learning the hard way that if a judge is inconvenienced by a case in Cleveland, he'll just get rid of it. They'll also act on working agreements with favored, local attorneys.

Opposing counsel was a tall and cadaverous presence named Chris Horn. Horn was on local boards in the affluent suburbs and spoke in stentorian tones. He understood that the rules of a legal system impose limits to the extent you could lie and divert good purpose.

I was still operating under the belief that judges, prosecutors, police and attorneys wanted to do right and would never distract a court from moral and ethical standards. Attorneys are sworn to uphold the intent of the law. We can't use rules to foil right and wrong. Judges would never favor one counsel over another. What A Dunce.

Chagrin Falls is served by Bedford Municipal Court. Bedford is a traditionally white, working class suburb whose population was replaced by a black contingent as the white people became more affluent and left. The city administration and judiciary remained white. Bedford, along with Parma, Ohio, are the two suburbs which bred, trained and maintained the most corrupt actors in the County.

The former Bedford Assistant Prosecutor and Law Director was named Tommy Longo. Longo was recently arrested in Mexico on a federal warrant for parole and weapons violations. His prior convictions included rape, weapon offenses and dealing drugs with local organized crime figures. He worked in the court during the tenure of Judge Peter Junkin, about whom I wrote the editorial in April of 2007.

Tom Day is the Bedford Clerk of Courts. He was indicted by a Cuyahoga County grand jury in 1986 on bribery and theft-in-office charges after he was accused of helping to fix cases in Cleveland Municipal Court. Common Pleas Judge John Angelotta dismissed the charges during Day's trial in February 1987, saying that the prosecution's main witness lied to get himself a lighter sentence. Day was also named as Public Official 13 in the recent indictment of County Commissioner Jimmy Dimora and was alleged to be helping find employment in the Bedford and Solon courts for women who provided sexual services to Dimora in exchange for work.

Joe Pfundstein is a Bedford magistrate who was found guilty of ethical violations before the Ohio Supreme Court Disciplinary Counsel. His license was suspended for a year with the suspension stayed on conditions that he remain on supervised probation and receive psychological treatment. Serious penalties were avoided when the other Bedford judge, Brian Melling, testified on his behalf.

Peter Junkin was the judge about whom I wrote a critical editorial. He was targeted by the FBI for activities with alleged members of the L.A. mafia. One of Junkin's associates was Russ Massetta. Russ' father-in-law is Peter Milano, former head of the L.A. mob. Junkin was later named in an indictment as a person who also arranged jobs in Bedford Municipal Court for the women with whom former County Commissioner DiMora had sex. Read the excerpt from the May 15, 2012 Cleveland Plain Dealer, below:

> "In another wiretap, Dimora called Tom Day, the clerk at Bedford Municipal Court. "Is Junkin alright with carrying her through until Solon works out?" Dimora asked Day, referring to former Judge Peter Junkin. Day replied "yes," and said Coppers would work in the clerk's office about three and a half days a week. Day also told Dimora she'd be able to make "what she wanted to make," which was $24,000 for a part-time job.
>
> Read more:http://www.newsnet5.com/dpp/news/political/ corruption_probe/evidence-released-on-jimmy-dimoras-affair- with-gina-coppers#ixzz2BsRAT6WN"

Junkin's wife, Jill, was appointed director for a cemetery of which Russ Massetta was president. The cemetery purchased stone from Massetta's company. Jill Junkin was being paid between $90,000.00 and $125,000.00 for what seemed to be a part-time endeavor. Junkin's stepson also serves on the cemetery board for $3,000.00 per year.

The former mayor of Bedford Hts. is named Jimmy DiMora. He was recently arrested, tried and sent to federal prison for bribery and corruption charges. Subsequent to being mayor, he became one of the three Cuyahoga County Commissioners and during that time maintained a standard of consumption which would challenge anyone's endocrine system. His indictment says Dimora received bribes and kickbacks, trips, home improvements and appliances, meals, entertainment, jewelry, lodging and prostitutes. In exchange, the charges state, Dimora steered government contracts, grants and loans, jobs and pay raises. He's also accused of fixing court cases and favoring his benefactors in dealings with the county.

Lead prosecutor Antoinette Bacon said Dimora and Russo "couldn't just put a cash register on their desk with a price list" but partnered up early in their political careers to gain power and control of Cuyahoga County.

The FBI had been planning a Cleveland sting since 2000, but didn't start arrests until spring of 2008; just months after I was targeted.

I sat in my catered cell waiting for "CT Bail-Bonds". He came 45 minutes later and was a sturdy African-American with a European style cap and an informal wisdom. We stood in front of the younger officer who accompanied me from Downtown and discussed my case. Bondsmen don't provide bail just because someone asks them. They have to assess their risks. I was an anomalous defendant. "You don't sound like you should be where you are". He winced as I described the events in terms of "laughable acts of corruption and lies", while the police were in the room.

"Baby, you don't have to say this in front of the police."

I paid him $367.00 and he filled out paperwork. I was released. Still time to make dinner with friends. He offered a ride to my destination. We approached his squashie Gremlin style hatch-back which was tended by a muscular friend in a fedora. They were both surprisingly cheerful and conversational. They reassured me about the future of my case and said it felt like it would "go away". The evanescence of the thought was benign. Evil would become diffused in the prevailing good of the world. We shook hands and I left the vehicle. Smiles all around.

After the holidays, I drove back to Vermont and looked up the charges against me. The nature of my alleged crime(s) required the element of proximity. One had to create the fear of imminent harm by virtue of making a geographically possible threat. I read some Ohio cases and found one about a police officer who was threatening his next door neighbor and showing her weapons. That proximity satisfied the statute. I called from Vermont. The distance did not satisfy the statute.

Oral statements have a real First Amendment problem. There is a strong presumption against limitations on speech. I was once threatened in Vermont by one of my tenants who spent time in prison for participating in a gun battle. I changed the screens in his apartment and he called at 5:00 in the morning to tell me he was going to break all my fingers;

"Do you hear me?" "I'M GOING TO BREAK EVERY BONE IN YOUR HAND!"

I held the receiver in my hand and stared at it.

"Are you there?" he wanted to know. "Don't ever go in my place. Are you listening? . . . say something."

I watched the phone a bit more and turned it off. I called the police who knew him.

"Guy's a real pain in the ass, but what did he do?

I told them he did nothing except for the call.

"Just one call's not enough. He has to DO something", said the officer.

It made sense. We have the right to raise our voices. This Ohio charge should be easy. I wasn't in Ohio at the time and the state couldn't prove the necessary elements of the crime. Plus, speech was involved which tends to be protected by the First Amendment. No one got hit. What I didn't understand was why the police and prosecutor didn't bring charges against the Condominium for criminal fraud and embezzlement. I actually filed my own Complaint with the Chagrin Falls police which was disregarded. They didn't care about a $76,000.00 theft.

I had to drive in from Vermont on February 13, 2008, to meet with prosecutor Tom Hanculak. A criminal trial is preceded by a pre-trial hearing. Prosecutors, defendants and attorneys meet to discuss the possibility of a settlement, trial and possible resolutions. I mistrusted him immediately. His protruding teeth gave him a look of demented contempt. He had a scripted style of speech like someone who learned manners to hide his true and bad intent. His adopted persona was a lie.

"Well Mr. Grundstein, in light of the circumstances, I really should ask for a special prosecutor."

Great idea. I was in the courthouse of the judge (Peter Junkin) about whom I wrote an editorial in 2007. There were only two judges for that jurisdiction and the one handling my case was not only Junkin's co-judge, but also his partner in private practice before they both became judges. Things like this don't happen by accident.

"Aren't we supposed to meet in front of the judge? The docket says the pre-trial is before J. Melling."

"Well, this is the way we do it here. I can ask for a special prosecutor if you like, but maybe you'd like to discuss other alternatives."

"O.K. You have my brief. I wasn't in state. I don't fit the criminal description. My behavior didn't meet the definition of a crime."

Tom thought a moment and asked me to wait in the corridor. He turned and went in a courtroom. He returned after 10 minutes.

"I'll tell you what I'll do, Mr. Grundstein. I'll have the charges dismissed if you waive all rights against us for abuse of process and other claims. It's a blanket waiver."

"O.K.. Will that end it? What about my bail? You guys cost me over $375.00 and a trip here."

"Well, if you want to go to trial, I'll just tell the judge." Tom turned and started to take large steps towards the courtroom.

"No. Hold on. I live in Vermont. Let's just end this. I'll take the deal. The case'll be dismissed, right?"

"Yup".

Tom left to enter a courtroom again (I was never invited) then returned with a piece of paper. He took large steps and moved his head in time with his walk like a cartoon character. I looked at the paper. It said I promise not to sue. I signed it. An illegible second signature was next to mine. It didn't have a typewritten name under it. .

"What about my bail? Can I get that back?"

Tom turned as he was walking away with his clipboard and our agreement which he gave to a court bailiff,

"Call the bail bondsman."

That was insulting. The bondsman wouldn't give me shit back. They kept 10% of each total bail amount. Since there were two charges (menacing and telephonic harassment) the bail was $1500.00 per charge for a total of $3,000.00. I had to pay $300.00 plus service fees.

I noticed a young bailiff shaking his head from side to side as he stared at me. He was suppressing a grin.

Oh well, it was over. It cost slightly over $350.00 and a trip from Vermont, but I got an entry of "Dismissed/Not Guilty". One less thing about which I had to worry during my felony adventure.

Maybe.

6

Family

The only thing I heard from my family since my arrest was that they planned on selling the house in which I lived. We had a family dwelling in Vermont which my father left to his four children.

I also discovered a family member acting as Trustee had embezzled $94,000.00 dollars (ninety four thousand) from my mother's trust account. The Trustee was also named Guardian with Power of Attorney. My mother was an elderly widow and suffered from Alzheimer's. This was the second family estate from which the Trustee committed financial misdeeds. The first was that of my aunt who died in the fall of 2000. Her will was not contested and other than the Trustee's violations, there was no need for litigation.

7

Prosecutor Bill Mason's 15 Siblings and 11 Pretrials

"Strangers don't matter"

The Cuyahoga County prosecutor was Bill Mason. Bill came from a Catholic family in Parma, Ohio and had 15 brothers and sisters. Although he was not Irish, he was able to win the support of the west side Irish Catholic political machine to become elected. The west side Irish had suffered a huge defeat when Stephanie Tubbs-Jones was elected prosecutor in 1991. She took the place of a man named Corrigan. A formidable negro woman from the East side had displaced the pale Hibernians from the west. The Irish promised themselves that another "outsider" would never hold so powerful a county position, especially when the position of prosecutor can be decisive with respect to judge elections. Mason was right to run the machine. County reform took place later, but county reform had nothing to do with reforming politics.

Bill's father was a union carpenter and his mother a nurse. Bill wrestled in high school and college and had the square face of a tough policeman. His oversized tongue and recessed mouth give him an unappealing sensuality. It's surprising to hear him lisp. Early in his political career, he lost an election and promised himself that would never happen again. He learned many things growing up in a house where the amount of available food was always uncertain. Being a member of the service class also taught him some lessons about power and control. The English inflicted some bitter lessons the West Siders didn't forget. You don't cooperate with others; you determine their decisions by controlling their alternatives. The history of Cromwell traveled to the New World.

Mason bragged that he had a conviction rate of 93%. About 15 thousand people were indicted each year. Over a period of 10 years, half the population of Cleveland would be indicted by a Grand Jury. The national conviction average is 68%. I learned how Bill got his high percentages. He had police lie to Grand Juries, hid exculpatory evidence, disregarded procedural rules and forced people to attend so many pre-trials they lost their jobs.

Bill Mason's illegal behaviors were documented in several newspaper articles (AFTER) the FBI raided the county. The articles included:

1. "Presumed Guilty: Prosecutions Without Evidence. How Bill Mason's Office Went After Hundreds of People With Little or No Evidence". Judges acquitted 364 people in midtrial without waiting for the defense to present its case. Cases include a person indicted for theft, even though he didn't take anything, a woman accused of stealing her own car after it turned up 50 miles away with a smashed windows and license plates belonging to a third party, a man prosecuted for drug dealing even though the police admitted they had no evidence of drugs or other wrongdoing and the prosecution of a Vermont resident for entering a court clerk's office in Cuyahoga county and altering an original document when he was working in New Hampshire at the time as proven by ATM receipts.

2. Mason job trading to get his brother a county position.

3. "Bill Mason's family tree plants deep roots in Cuyahoga County jobs."

During Mason's two-decade career in politics, taxpayers have paid his relatives more than $2.2 million in salary, a Plain Dealer review of public payrolls and other records has found. Thirteen of Mason's family members are employed by the county. An additional five are employed by his home town of Parma, Ohio and three more work for the state. The total is 21. Many of these were for jobs that weren't publicly advertised. Voters in adjacent Summit County passed a 2006 law that bans relatives of top officials from receiving county jobs.

Most disturbing are the number of criminals who contributed to Mason's campaign treasury.

See "Cleveland Scene" article "Feeding the Machine", October 22, 2008;

WHO GIVES:

*Frank Mahnic: Convicted in 1996 for giving false information to a grand jury. Contributions: $10,150.

*Carole Hoover: Ran a minority-owned company involved in an airport expansion project that never paid county taxes during Mike White's administration. Contributions: $9,500.

*Sam Miller: Forest City executive whose subsidiary, Sunrise Developments, bought contaminated land and sold it to the county for a profit of about $2 million. Contributions: $7,500.

*John and Ferris Kleem: Owners of Blaze Construction, whose office was raided by the FBI in July. Contributions: $3,250.

*Russell Masetta: Founder of Nature Stone flooring. According to news reports, Masetta married the daughter of the Los Angeles mafia's boss and took a job there, working for the Teamsters. He was arrested in 1988 after accepting a bribe from an FBI agent (he was charged with a felony but pleaded guilty to a misdemeanor and spent four months behind bars). His local business was named in an FBI search warrant during the recent county raids, apparently because Nature Stone did work on the palatial homes of Jimmy Dimora and Frank Russo. It's not clear whether Nature Stone was visited by agents. Contributions: $7,500.

*John Allega: Owner of Allega Cement Contractors, a company that was suspended from doing business with Cleveland in 2007 after an investigation found that Allega was using minority front companies to win a contract at Cleveland Hopkins International Airport. Contributions: $3,850.

*William Schatz: Attorney who worked part-time for the sewer district at a salary of $160,000 while also representing companies that won sewer contracts. He resigned last year after a sewer-district board member started asking questions. Contributions: $4,300.

*Ricardo Teamor: A close ally to former mayor Mike White, he admitted to bribing former Councilman Joe Jones to get city contracts and served four months in prison. Contributions: $1,000.

*James Palladino: A felon (last convicted in 1972) and a target in a 1989 FBI investigation into drug smuggling (that did not lead to charges), he once ran the area's most lucrative garbage business before moving to Kelleys Island. Contributions: $1,000.

*Steve Pumper: CEO of D-A-S Construction. His home and business were raided by the FBI earlier this year. It appears he did about $50,000 worth of construction on Jimmy Dimora's house. Contributions: $1,350.

*Andrew Futey: Republican lobbyist who got probation for his role in laundering campaign contributions to state Treasurer Joe Deters for stock broker Frank Gruttadauria. Contributions: $2,000.

*William Consolo: A developer who gave Parma Mayor Dean DePiero free office space for his campaign and hired a company owned by DePiero's family as its leasing agent, while DePiero voted in favor of a $8.5 million office park built by Consolo's company. Contributions: $2,850.

*Jason Lucarelli: Runs the Minute Men day laborers business with his father, Sam, who pleaded guilty to racketeering charges in 1989 after the FBI uncovered his side business, a local gambling ring. Contributions: $9,500.

Employees of Bill Mason have also donated $82,885 to his campaign.

WHO GETS from Mason's campaign treasury:

*State Attorney General, Richard Cordray: $10,000

*Gov. Ted Strickland: $10,000

*The Ohio Democratic Party: $30,000

*Pat O'Malley, Mason's college roommate and convicted pervert: $15,000 loan to his campaign fund.

*Carol Mason, Bill Mason's wife: $2,825.75 for "computer input," "letter service" and "consulting."

*Ridgewood Golf Course, Parma's public golf course. **When then-state Auditor Jim Petro's office audited the golf course in 1999, it found alarming signs of a money-laundering operation in the works**; cash registers that were opened 4,000 times when there was no record of a transaction, 330 late bank deposits, and missing financial records and receipts. **At the time the books were allegedly cooked, Jack Krise was Parma's treasurer**, and Michael Mason, Bill's brother, was his deputy treasurer. Krise is now a fiscal affairs officer in Bill Mason's office. $50,505, plus $1,160 in "cash gratuities."

*Kelly Mason, Mason's daughter: $2,090 for "campaign work" and a "donation."

*Tom Regas, a Parma councilman who currently works in the county engineer's office and writes the checks for Mason's campaign fund: $8,050 for "consulting" and "catering."

*Thousands of dollars were spent on graduation gifts for the sons and daughters of employees and contributors, though no one made out as nicely as Tom Regas' daughters, who each got $250.

*Thousands more were spent on wedding presents for staffers and political allies, including Ryan Miday, Mason's spokesman, who got a $150 check on his big day.

*Mason's Mean Machine, pee-wee football league: $3,600 for "uniforms."

(Sources: Friends of Bill Mason campaign finance reports (2002-2008), The Plain Dealer, the Columbus Dispatch, Black Box Voting.org, Scene.)

Some of Mason's critics say that reflects what they call the prosecutor's hypocrisy and arrogance: How could Mason push thousands of routine criminal cases through the court system while apparently overlooking widespread corruption among his friends and political allies over the past decade?

Many critics have been afraid to speak openly about their concerns for fear Mason — the most powerful Democrat left standing in the wake of the county corruption investigation — could retaliate, hurting both their professional and political futures.

When a party is indicted and arraigned, the prosecutor schedules a pre-trial. My first was set for January of 2008. I was elated and was sure they'd acknowledge all my exculpatory evidence. It was easy to see that I wasn't even in Ohio at the time charged on the indictment and that I got a "No Bill" from the Grand Jury on the first presentment. A "No Bill" terminates prosecution in favor of the accused. This was confirmed by the case of "Froehlich v Ohio Board of Mental Health" which was released by the Ohio Supreme Court a week before my indictment was signed by the Grand Jury.

I read the statute under which I was indicted. It had misdemeanor and felony provisions. The felony provisions pertained to alteration of a will or for changing an original court document or record under the control and in the possession of the court clerk. I didn't alter a will. The indictment didn't mention anything about a will. I had no access to original court documents if I wasn't in Ohio. All the other sections were misdemeanor offenses. The misdemeanor statute of limitations in Ohio is 2 years. My indictment was dated August 2007 and said I committed a 2nd degree felony in April of 2003, but it was impossible if I wasn't in Ohio at the time and any possible behaviors were not felonies. The statute of limitations had passed over two years ago. I was sure we'd have a laugh over this and I'd go home without further concern.

During December and January, I filed several motions to dismiss based on the alibi defense that I was not in Ohio at the time charged and that the statute of limitations had expired. Everyone would acknowledge this was all a mistake. The prosecutor didn't answer any of my motions and the judge would not rule on them.

Rule 40 of the Ohio Rules for Superintendence of the Courts says that a court must rule on a motion within 120 days. The assigned judge never ruled on any motions over a period of 11 months.

I drove through a hard snow storm for the first pre-trial. Cars trundled through the interstate burdened by snow and directed through pie shaped sectors cut by windshield wipers. They looked like strange, mobile meringues. The prosecutor was represented by an assistant prosecutor who asked if I wanted to settle and accept a misdemeanor conviction. I said absolutely not. He didn't want to discuss my defenses or alibi evidence. He didn't mention any obligation to acknowledge them. The equities of the case didn't matter to him. Did I want to settle or not? If not, the meeting is over. When I asked about "Brady" obligations, he said there were none in Cuyahoga County. There is no open discovery and the prosecutor could withhold whatever evidence he wanted prior to trial.

"Brady v Maryland" 373 US 83, is a case that requires a prosecutor to reveal and acknowledge all exculpatory evidence in favor of the accused. It's designed to prevent a prosecutor from using an unfair advantage to force an outcome. Cuyahoga County not only disregarded "Brady", but also had a rule which allowed the prosecution to edit evidence in its possession and which exempted it from turning over original documents if it felt doing so would jeopardize a Grand Jury or other witness. The prosecution would read what it thought was safe to reveal from its file to defense attorney, who could take notes or dictation. This outrage allowed the prosecution to hide evidence, which it did on a regular basis.

It's common for the parties who populate legal administrations to interpret rules in a way that contradict the intent of American jurisprudence. You always run into some rock-head or opportunist who will say, "but the rule says this" when asked to acknowledge that enforcement of the rule will do more damage than non-enforcement in a particular situation. Good people and bad people use the same rules. Their intent varies. Written law is only evidence of our culture of fairness and is subject to interpretation consistent with our notions of right and wrong. "Equity follows the law", is another expression of this principle. Equity concerns the moral content which is used to elicit the meaning of law. It's wrong when statutes are applied without reference to their intent.

Statutory law exists to remove the uncertainty of legal interpretation from judge to judge in contrast to common law or case law which is designed to adapt to the discrete equities of every fact situation. Statutes are written when a legislature has decided a certain set of facts needs its own, ascertained remedy and the conditions for which the statute is designed are too important for a wide range of interpretation and uncertain adjudication. However, they are still subject to interpretation with respect to their intent and are strictly interpreted to limit their application. Ambiguities in statutes are resolved in favor of an accused.

Cuyahoga county prosecutors had a self-serving rule which violated every notion of equity and fairness we have. You can't trust humans with that kind of evidentiary advantage. Prosecutors are happy to bring bad charges to show "they get results."

As a species, we value those who represent income, power, preferential association and sex. Non-functional commitments are rare. Your mother loves you . . . if you're lucky. Defendants can be more useful as parties to injure than those whose rights should be respected. What's a little unfair sentence here and there if an assistant can use them to get a promotion? No one ever says anything. No one cares.

I sat there like a torn paper bag. I wasn't ready for this peremptory treatment by the prosecutor. He wasn't interested in my defenses and blandly left after I refused a plea. This wasn't fair. I came from Vermont. Didn't they respect my time, responsible motions and innocence? Well, no. They were using geography against me.

I drove back to Vermont and looked at the docket 3 days later. The docket said I'd asked for a continuance to perform "more discovery". I never asked for a continuance. I asked to have the case dismissed. I looked up the procedures for continuance in the local court rules. Rule 23(h) says a continuance request has to be signed by the party requesting it. The signature of his/her attorney is not sufficient.

I didn't want a continuance or more discovery. I didn't sign anything. I later learned that the prosecutor arranged with the clerk's office to have a default setting by which requests for continuances are assigned to defendants. When a defendant asks for a continuance, he tolls the time within which his trial must take place. In Ohio, a 1st degree misdemeanor trial must take place within 90 days. A felony trial must take place within 270 days. See ORC 2945.71. Not only was I not in Ohio on or near the time alleged on the second indictment, (April, 2003) but the the statute of limitations (2 years for a misdemeanor, 6 years for a felony) had passed almost 3 years prior in 2005. Now they also want to foil my right to a speedy trial.

Another pre-trial was set for two weeks later. I called the bailiff who worked for the judge. Bailiffs are like a judge's personal administrative assistant and are the face of the court. I asked if I could have a pre-trial by phone. She angrily denied that possibility and snarled that if I didn't arrive in person, a warrant for my arrest would be issued. This wasn't going well.

I drove in a second time at which the procedure was repeated. The prosecutor asked if I wanted to take a plea and I refused. No one responded to my motions and the judge didn't rule on any of them.

I decided to hire an attorney. It didn't make a difference. I had to drive in twice more. Each time the meetings took about 5 minutes and the attorney told me he was asked if I wanted to take a plea. It took me longer to tie my tie than participate in these pre-trials. I always declined a settlement. After each pre-trial, a docket entry was made saying I asked for a continuance to discover more evidence. They must have a default setting organized by the prosecutor which entered fraudulent data. This wasn't a legal system, it was people using their access to the police power and unfair advantage to force an illegal outcome.

Three years later, the Clerk of the Criminal Court docket was fired in September of 2011 and arraigned in October of 2012 for stealing money and tampering with records. See the "Cleveland Plain Dealer" excerpt, directly below:

> Cleveland Plain Dealer/September 28, 2012:
> "Mark Lime, 57, who ran the office's criminal division for nine years, was indicted by a grand jury on two theft-related counts and 72 others of tampering with evidence and unauthorized use of property."

I received a call from my attorney during the last week in February, 2008. He wanted to tell me about the arrest warrant issued against me. The court scheduled a pre-trial and my attorney forgot to tell me about it. He called to give me notice of the hearing after its scheduled time had passed. Attendance is obligatory at pre-trials. If a defendant doesn't appear, an arrest warrant is issued. We had to move to have the warrant recalled. The judge's bailiff was spitting nails. I hated this.

Between December and February of 2008, I made five trips to Ohio.

Trial was set for March 11, 2008.

FBI

I decided to call the FBI. They put me in touch with someone named "Analyst Christine" who called in Vermont. She conducted a phone interview and asked for a written statement. I sent a detailed description which seemed to be absorbed by the agency. "Christine" and I had a brief email correspondence, after which she disappeared into the opaque fabric of federal investigations. I never heard from her again. There were no expressions of gratitude, understanding or sympathy. However, there was also no hostility nor did they arrest me. I expected moral outrage. Instead, the whole thing was very low affect.

I was sure the FBI would mobilize and vindicate me immediately. It didn't. I contributed to a data base after which I was assigned a priority. A low one. The complete silence which followed indicated my contribution to the agency was done. It also meant the agency would offer no protection . . . or gratitude.

8

Menacing II; Tuffy Joe O'Malley and the Right Catholic Schools

"Former prosecutor Joe O'Malley, 45, felt that he would not be safe at the Federal Prison in Morgantown, W. VA, after testifying against all his co-defendants in exchange for sentence reduction"

A prosecutor named Joe O'Malley called me in late February of 2008. He said he was responsible for bringing charges against me in Parma, Ohio municipal court. When I asked him what those charges were, he explained that they were for telephonic harassment and menacing. He wanted to try the Bedford case again.

The statutory provisions, (ORC 2917.21(A)(3) and 2903.2 (ORC 2917.21(A)(3) and 2903.21), were identical to those filed in Bedford Municipal Court for which there was already a disposition of "Not Guilty/Case Dismissed" on the docket. I promised to fax him all the details and proof of disposition in a prior court. Joe said he'd look into it and I could call him later. I sent him a 12 page fax and waited a week to see what he'd decided.

There should have been no ambiguity. The Bedford judgment was *res judicata* and double jeopardy against a new prosecution. I'd already been arrested and posted bail. I traveled to Ohio for a pre-trial where Tom Hanculak and I signed a plea agreement. The matter was over. Plus plea agreements act as a contract with the state. They couldn't bring the same charges again. The Bedford prosecutor, Hanculak, and I had a deal. The state can't breach its contract. I couldn't keep driving to Ohio. I was going broke and I had already been there five times in three months..

There was also the issue of venue. If criminal charges are incorrectly brought in the wrong location, Ohio Rule of Criminal Procedure 18, states the procedure for moving the case to the correct venue. A motion or notice to transfer venue is made, the original bail is carried over to the new venue and the case is moved to another court in the jurisdiction where the crime was alleged to have happened. Venue, unlike Subject Matter Jurisdiction, is waivable, and if parties agree to a determination in the wrong venue, that determination is binding. My determination was an entry of "Not Guilty/Case Dismissed" in Bedford Municipal Court. The case was over.

I called O'Malley a week later. I got the same low affect persona.

"Hi Joe, did you have a chance to look at the Bedford docket sheets I sent? You should be able to dismiss this, right?

"Yeah, well, I don't know, but we're taking the case. You'll have to come in and make bail."

"But Joe, what about all the stuff I sent you. It's not hard to understand. I was found "Not Guilty"/Case Dismissed". Is there something I'm missing about Ohio procedure?"

"Uh, we want this case to go through."

"Joe, I understand you want this case to go through, but can you address my defenses? Maybe I'm missing something."

"You can bring this stuff up with the judge."

"Joe, you control the case. You're the prosecutor. You could dismiss this if you wanted. I've given you excellent grounds to get rid of the case. I'm not only innocent, but it was dismissed in another court. How can you bring the case again?"

"You can get an attorney."

We hung up. I looked out the window into the relentless and dense cold of winter. These extra charges would add another two to five trips to Ohio over the course of a year and jeopardized my reputation with respect to the ongoing felony charges. If a judge found I was a serial offender, I'd never get out of jail and would be fined into oblivion.

Joe didn't care. His persona expressed no particular view of life. He was whatever he needed to be for anyone who provided income.

Joe was actually imprisoned four years later after being arrested and convicted of case fixing and lying to the FBI during its Cuyahoga county corruption investigations. That didn't do me any good during February of 2008, prior to the big FBI raids, but it still vindicated my posture with respect to Joe's prosecution.

Turns out Joe had a working relation with County Auditor Frank Russo, County Commissioner DiMora and a couple judges who were also sent to jail. During the Auditor's trial, Russo testified that Joe would give him $5,000.00 campaign donations in exchange for contract steering.

The judges with whom Joe had special relations included Common Pleas judge Stephen Terry and Bridget McCafferty. Bridget and Joe were classmates at St. Angela's Catholic School in Fairview Park, Ohio.

McCafferty was made a candidate for judge and elected to office straight out of law school. She never even tried a case prior to her election.

The "Cleveland Plain Dealer" documented the preferential relation Joe had with Bridget:

"Over the last 21 months, O'Malley appeared before McCafferty on behalf of poor defendants up to six times as often as he did before 32 of the 33 other Judges in the Common Pleas Court.

Neither Kevin Spellacy (O'Malley's attorney) nor Chief Judge Nancy McDonnell could explain Friday how 26 of McCafferty's cases became assigned to O'Malley, given that cases involving needy clients are supposed to be divided evenly among interested defense lawyers.

The assignments are made by judges at arraignments held daily. The 34 judges take turns presiding over the arraignments."

Ex Judge McCafferty was sent to jail for lying to the FBI during the County Corruption investigation. Ex Judge Terry was sent to jail for fixing a case on behalf of O'Malley and lying about it to the FBI.

Parma, the Mason Axis

As I mentioned, the FBI raids gave me no leverage in late February of 2008. I had to comply with Joe's agenda. The new jurisdiction where the crimes were alleged to have occurred was North Royalton, Ohio. The court for N. Royalton is Parma Ohio Municipal Court; County Prosecutor Bill Mason's hometown and the place where he got his political start. Mason had long standing ties with the Parma Law Director, Tim Dobeck who hired Mason's daughter as a law clerk, a position that was not publicly advertised or posted. Mason's wife even worked in Parma Municipal Court.

Bail is set by the police detective who drafted the criminal complaint and presented charges to a prosecutor. In this case the detective was John Barsa. That meant I had to call N. Royalton. My call was taken by the desk officer. She said the detective wasn't available, but she'd ask the watch commander how I should proceed. I held for a couple minutes while she spoke with someone in the station. When she returned, she said they wanted $350.00 bail for each charge. That's odd.

How did they figure that out? Normally bail is 10% of a total. Did they want $3,500.00 per alleged offense? Did N. Royalton want a $7,000.00 bail obligation for an offense which was dismissed? Otherwise, a total bail of $350.00 per charge wasn't worth the trouble. Unless this was a shakedown.

I asked how I could pay it. Could I send a check? I was told they didn't accept checks and must pay cash. Since my trial on the Felony charge was set for March 11, I figured I'd drive in early and pay the bond in N. Royalton on my way to downtown Cleveland where my Felony case was to be tried. The desk officer promised it would take five minutes and I could go immediately. It was a routine transaction and police weren't involved. A clerk could take the money and do the paperwork. It would all take place in the lobby of the N. Royalton police station.

It all sounded very banal for an illegal prosecution. I felt better. N. Royalton was going to be blown out of its zip code on a case like this. No judge would support this kind of extortion and procedural incompetence. All I had to do was file a motion to dismiss and Parma would dismiss the case with an apology to me.

I was learning quickly that the legal system is like a political system and works on the basis of personal relations. Never mind disciplined intellectual analysis and abstractions. Likeable people who make business transactions easy do well. That meant I had to get a local attorney. Someone who was really connected. I called around to ask who might be best suited for Parma Municipal Court. Two names came up, Bob Sindyla and Kevin Spellacy.

Bob Sindyla was the former prosecutor for N. Royalton. He'd be perfect for a charge from N. Royalton. When I called, Bob answered from the locker room of a country club. He was getting ready for a golf outing. I told him of my happenstance and Bob said he knows everybody. As a matter of fact, the judge who would be hearing the case was in the locker room with him, right then. We agreed to speak later.

I sent my file and called him again. He was friendly and reassuring when we discussed the charges. I said nothing like this had ever happened to me and the offenses made me look bad. Bob laughed and said he defends people who are much worse than me; much worse. Bob sent some forms for me to sign which I returned with the retainer check. Bob said if we did it right, I wouldn't even have to come to Cleveland for a trial. We could make a plea agreement or have it dismissed. He knew the prosecutor and said he was "a reasonable guy". Seemed like this would be painless and low risk.

Several weeks later, I received a check from Bob's office and a letter. The check was written on Bob's business account for the amount of the retainer. It was a refund. The letter told me that Bob decided he couldn't represent me. There was no explanation. I called to ask why. Bob wasn't available. I just had to accept the letter.

I then called Kevin Spellacy. Who would be better than an Irish Catholic in a town run by Irish Catholics? The Spellacy name is all over Cleveland and included judges Margaret and Leo Spellacy. Kevin had been the law director for the suburb of Lakewood, Ohio. He was very friendly when I called. We spoke about the case and possible resolutions. He told me not to worry. He'd send a copy of his retainer agreement and we would talk again.

A week later, I received an email from Kevin. It said;

"Lose my name and phone number. Never call me again. Do not respond to this email."

As it turned out, Joe O'Malley, the prosecutor who brought charges against me, was being investigated by the FBI in the first subpoenas served by the Federal authorities in what would be a massive raid on the public administration of Cleveland, Ohio. His attorney was Kevin Spellacy. Joe knew exactly who was driving this thing against me.

I tried a third attorney who specialized in criminal law. We discussed the facts of my case and its history. He said it seemed very suspicious and remarked that Judge Lillian Greene committed outrageous offenses on a regular basis. He needed to speak with his partner. I called back a week later and he was apologetic.

"I spoke with my partner. He says this makes no sense at all. He's never seen this kind of relentless and aggressive activity for such a small offense against an out-of-state defendant. Somebody very powerful, or a group of somebodies, are chasing you. We cannot touch this case. Please don't use my name."

I tried another of the most prominent criminal defense attorneys in Cleveland. He wanted a $5,000.00 retainer. I didn't have it and was quickly going broke. Sindyla only needed $750.00. All the attorneys with whom I spoke said this was a small matter which could be dismissed or negotiated with an innocuous pleas agreement. I probably wouldn't even have to go to Ohio.

Now I did.

More Family

"Anti-Semeetes"

It was odd to sit across from my siblings in court. They brought a partition action to sell my Vermont residence. We didn't need to sell it. There was no mortgage on it. In addition, it was created in generosity and benevolence. Its presence was the best expression of nature and human character. It was built for my father by a mannish lesbian who loved him and his family. She worked for a dollar an hour just for the pleasure of giving and the continuing relation between her and my dad. Her ancestors had been in Vermont since the late 1700s. Thelma used to take me fishing and give me wisdom. "You don't make money from friends".

It was a beautiful, Adirondack style cabin built on a slope so it was among the tops of trees. It was part of the benevolent forest and fjord like lake on which it was built.

Subsequent to the hearing, their attorney made a motion to have me excluded from the property "so nothing could interfere with its marketing". The judge granted the request. My siblings could go there, but I couldn't.

Saved by the Blonde at The North Star Motel

I used the North Star Motel in Shelburne, Vermont as a stopping place on the way from Ohio. It was a good place to collapse after long drives which tended to start in the late morning after failed pre-trial meetings. Shelly Vinal owned the place and had an active curiosity about the people who came through. She also practiced a natural generosity. It was common for guests to give her flowers

It was something of a bargain motel and the staff wasn't stable. The employees who did show up on a regular basis tended to suffer from a variety of benign character defects and laziness. But it was a fun place and the guests were eclectic. They included travelers from Montreal, Mexican workers hired as contract laborers and itinerant hay mowers who would come in the spring.

Shelly would often leave prepared food in my room and make special things available from the motel freezer. After helping Shelly with a variety of small legal matters and repairs, she spontaneously invited me to stay at the motel on a permanent basis. A random act which provided exactly what I needed.

I spent the winter in Room 25, under the protection of blonde Shelly and sustained by the ample, continental breakfasts.

Felony Trial

*"You cannot have an organization without lies,
deceit and theft by those in control"*

The Ohio felony trial was set for March 11, 2008. I refused to take a plea and was sure I'd be vindicated at trial. The judge, Michael Russo, used to be a prosecutor, but everyone said he was very fair. I was learning that fair had little to do with anything any more. The legal system was about controlling the mechanism and determining outcomes for personal and group interest.

After four months, the prosecutor had answered none of my motions and the judge hadn't ruled on any of them. I am quite communicative and moved to dismiss on every legal basis available to me. These included;

1) my alibi excuse that I was not in Ohio at the time alleged on the indictment and couldn't have committed a crime in Ohio,

2) absence of Territorial Jurisdiction if I wasn't in Ohio,

3) the events described on the indictment didn't match the state's evidence which was only described a misdemeanor under the statute used by the police, for which the statute of limitations had passed,

4) double jeopardy (these events were actually scrutinized in Lakewood Municipal court 4 years earlier. The Lakewood court could not articulate an offense against me. It even went to the local appellate court where J. Karpinski screamed at the prosecutor for hauling me into Ohio without a cognizable offense.)

5) The "No Bill" I received from the Grand Jury was decisive with respect to this prosecution. Ohio law ("Froehlich v Ohio Board of Mental Health") says a "No Bill" terminates prosecution in favor of an accused and

6) the rule of lenity which says ambiguities in a statute are interpreted in favor of an accused and against the state. This is a rule of statutory interpretation.

The fact that I wasn't in Ohio at the time alleged in the indictment in conjunction with the original "No Bill" should have been decisive. Only four per cent of parties before a Grand Jury get "No Bills". It's easier to find fault than absence of fault with a Grand Jury. But I could get no response from anyone. The prosecutor disregarded my exculpatory evidence and legal argument. Mason seemed satisfied using geography against me until I did what he wanted.

The Quiet Extortion of Pleas
"We just don't care about your defenses"

I spoke with an attorney who did criminal defense. He said it was common for Bill Mason to schedule lots of pre-trials to make a defendant miss work. People are normally fired after the 5th pre-trial and can't afford to maintain a defense, even if they are innocent. Mason's bragged of a 95% conviction rate. The national average was between 60 and 70 %. It was really a 95% extortion rate.

Since this was my first experience with serious criminal charges, I still was sure the prosecution wanted to do the right thing. I hadn't learned yet that Cuyahoga county had exempted itself from the Constitutional culture of the U.S. and its duty to acknowledge exculpatory evidence. "Brady v Maryland" 373 US 83, was a landmark case in which the US Supreme Court held that withholding exculpatory evidence violates due process "where the evidence is material either to guilt or to punishment". Prosecutor Mason knew I wasn't in Ohio on or near the time alleged, he knew I got a "No Bill", he knew I never altered an original court document or committed fraud on a court. But he wouldn't act on his knowledge. I was being squeezed by the vice of geography, travel costs and my diminishing reputation.

Hearing and Arrest for Breakfast

My trial was set for Monday, March 11. I hired an attorney to help me with the hearing. He did very little and used all the motions and documents I filed previously. He too didn't understand why this case was going forward.

Early March can be a miserable seasonal transition in Vermont. It's a time for ice storms which coat roads, trees and cars. You can't even walk on paved surfaces. Trees and electric lines collapse and neighborhoods are cluttered with fallen items. It's an ambiguous look in which elegantly coated debris is illuminated with the new light of early spring.

An enormous ice storm hit N. Vermont the weekend prior to my trial. Roads were closed all over the state. The storm developed the Thursday before and I called J. Russo's office to ask for a continuance. The bailiff shouted that no continuance would be allowed and that I would be arrested if I didn't appear. Her tone was appropriate for a Concentration camp. I sent weather maps and state police reports with closed roads. It didn't matter. The bailiff said I better be there.

I also had the matter of posting bail in N. Royalton for the O'Malley charges. I called the police and said I'd arrive very early in the morning of the 10th. I didn't tell them I was going to attend a felony trial later during business hours. They reassured me and said there was always someone there.

I left early Sunday morning to make sure I'd arrive in Ohio on time. The trip would be longer than usual since I had to avoid closed roads, but I became accustomed to the plodding drive to the midwest. I even learned my favorite places to stop for gas and goodies.

A franchise called "Stewarts" has locations in NY and S. Vermont. It has its own anachronistic aesthetic which is supra-personal and abstract in a '50s kind of way. "Stewarts" offers a lot of its own products for sale so their stores have less of the in-store displays provided by large manufactures like Coca-cola, etc. They draw attention to their ice cream, coffee, baked goods, hot dogs, cold beverages and sandwiches by locating signs in a pleasant script all over the store. This script was not connected to any contemporary, garish and shrill marketing identities created by large manufacturers, but created the effect of what an individual who owned a road-stop along route 66 before the interstates opened, would like to draw attention to the items she made for sale. I loved it there. Not only did they offer two hot dogs for $1.99 (which included a relish bar and hot chile at no extra charge), but they had streusel crumb cake in polite paper holders, unincarcerated by a hermetically tight wrap of cling-film. I mean, streusel is powerful stuff and capable of diverting, for an interval, all the anxiety of felony charges. I would stop for things I didn't need or when I wasn't hungry just to experience the uncluttered persona of their commercial aesthetic.

I made my way delicately through Vermont and up the eastern slope of the Adirondacks. The roads alternated between snow and slush at lower elevations to hard ice and powder on the peaks. I napped at a rest stop outside of Rochester and awoke at 2 a.m. to finish the trip. I would arrive in N. Royalton around 7:00 a.m. Plenty of time to change and drive to downtown Cleveland.

The N. Royalton police station is very accessible from the interstate. I arrived and entered a relatively new geometric structure with an ample lobby area and a large bank of bullet proof windows, one of which had an aperture for communication. A young officer with an ear cuff was staffing the window. This seemed promising. The young, the hip, the Generation X police. I announced my purpose and was asked for the bail amount. I paid it in seven 100 dollar bills. I asked if I could leave but was told to wait for a couple minutes during which I looked at police memorabilia in a display case located in the lobby. I went to the wash room and stood a bit longer.

A short, thick police officer was buzzed through the security door and said we'd have to go in the back where we'd do some paper work. This seemed odd. Why was a police officer involved. They said they would just take bail and write a receipt. I wasn't in a position to argue and went back through the security door with him where I was arrested. We went back to the small holding cells in the department where my clothing and shoes were taken. I was photographed, fingerprinted and booked. The officer had small, tense features and a mouth that looked like a sphincter. His Slavic name was "Vozar" or something. A terrible feeling with which I was becoming very familiar returned. He was organizing his thoughts as I asked him questions.

"Why am I being arrested? I've provided bail."

The officer tried to suppress a smile,

"Well, you have two offenses with bail of $350.00 each, but you gave us seven $100 dollar bills."

"And?"

"Um, we need two separate payments of $350.00. We don't make change."

The officer made spitting noises as he suppressed his laughter.

Jesus, the entire county of Cleveland was in on this. That made four sets of police, (Solon, Cuyahoga County Sheriff, Chagrin Falls, N. Royalton) three prosecutors (Mason, Hanculak, O'Malley), three judges (Junkin, Russo, Spanagel) and a court bailiff acting with knowledge of an agenda against me.

I became visibly distressed. Saddened. I had to be at trial in 1 1/2 hours. They knew this. I became insulting.

"Can I see the watch commander? He should know that some asshole is working a lie."

"He's not in yet. If you want to do this the hard way, we can do that too." said the officer.

He continued to ask questions needed to complete forms for intake. I sat there in handcuffs and prison slippers, watching the clock. They put me in a holding cell.

After a half hour, the watch commander (or someone) appeared. They decided to do a favor for me. They made a special dispensation and organized change for a Hundred dollar bill. I was given my clothes back and drove frantically to the Justice Center. I stopped at a service station to put on my tie. It took longer to find a place to park than it did to drive from N. Royalton.

The justice center opens at 8:30 and my trial was at 9:00 on the 17th floor. I arrived just as the building opened and stood in the large crowd of primarily underclass African Americans and dreary white people. Attorneys were distinguishable by their ties, brief cases and purposeful movement through the facility.

We went through the revolving doors and into the banded security line which organized people into a single file past the X-ray conveyor belts, the plastic holders into which metal items were placed and the metal detectors. Our things emerged from the x-ray scanners and accumulated in a pile at the exit end of the conveyors. You had to move fast to retrieve your change and keys. A large police desk faced the inspection area, but it was impossible to guarantee that someone wouldn't take a tempting item from a plastic dish that wasn't theirs. I had actually been cornered by two guys in the justice center elevator asking for cash. There wasn't enough time for a real shake-down in an express elevator that arrived at its destination in a matter of seconds.

Thousands of people came through here every day and many offenses were set for "cattle-call" misdemeanor and arraignment hearings at which 50-60 defendants sat in a large court room waiting for their turn before a judge. I took the elevator which bypassed the lower levels to service floors 11-19. It opened across from an identical bank of elevator doors. I turned left into the corridor which had courts and conference rooms on either side of it. Two large galleries of plastic seats were filled by people waiting for hearings. There were many infants, children and senior people. It looked as if some people brought their entire kinship group for emotional support and baby-sitting. A large bank of windows facing East illuminated the far end of the corridor. You could look out and see Lake Erie, wind generators and midtown Cleveland.

I was assigned a courtroom at the end of the corridor, closest to the windows. It had two sets of substantial double doors which opened from the center. A sign was taped to the door which said, "Do Not Enter. Court in Session". It was still before 9:00 and I went in. I was scheduled for 9:00. Nothing starts before 9:00. The courtroom was empty, so I sat by the large windows and waited for my attorney to arrive. I continued to wait until 9:30 and 10:00.

Nothing happened.

I went into the courtroom several times to check in or prove I was here. There was no staff in the courtroom. I walked up and down and worried intensely. Around 10:30, I saw some people I recognized. The bailiff, Mary Pat Smith, walked by me and said nothing. I saw some of the witnesses I subpoenaed on my behalf walk into a conference room, followed by my attorney. J. Russo appeared for a moment in robes. The assistant prosecutor was there. No one said anything to me. No one looked at me or addressed me. Not even my attorney.

I waited for another hour. During this time the same people went in and out of the conference room. I went in the courtroom where the bailiff was sitting. She looked up then back down to her desk. No one acknowledged my presence or said anything to me about scheduling. Not even my attorney.

The corridor cleared for lunch. I remained alone until 1:00 when the waiting area filled for afternoon hearings. I chatted with elderly gentlemen and some defendants who assumed I was an attorney and asked for advice. I gave it to them. It was gratifying. I went in and out of J. Russo's courtroom several times. Nothing seemed to be scheduled for it that day. There was no activity. At 4:00 I went to the prosecutor's office to ask what was going on. This was quite a legal faux pas, because the prosecutor is not allowed to speak with a represented defendant. The administrator looked at the departmental day book and said they had nothing scheduled for me. At 4:30 I was asked to leave the building. I went to J. Russo's courtroom one last time. It was empty. I gingerly left the Justice Center and drove home.

On the way back, I hit a deer outside the town of Speculator, NY, and ruined my hood, fender and right headlight.

I checked the docket two weeks later. It said the trial had been canceled (continued) at my request. I had still not heard from my attorney.

Soggy White People Receive Ohio Letter

"You just cannot trust the mail anymore"

Shortly prior to hearing I received a call from Seattle. A pleasant sounding man named Doug Ende said he represented the Washington State Bar, of which I was a member. He needed to speak with me about an anonymous letter they received from Cleveland. A "Concerned Citizen" wrote the bar to tell them of my indictment. There was no return address, office or name associated with it.

I thanked Mr. Ende for calling and told him I had nothing to hide and actually wanted as many people as possible to know what was happening to me.

He seemed satisfied and we parted cordially.

I assumed that was the last I would hear from the Bar.

Foreclosure

"You don't cooperate with people you can outmaneuver"
Attorney Rule #1

I was subject to a foreclosure action concurrent with the Cleveland criminal charges.

I purchased a condominium in the Cleveland suburb of Chagrin Falls as an investment during the time I was in Ohio taking care of my elderly parents. As it turned out, an act of family loyalty provided the means by which I became exposed to the catastrophic risks of the local judiciary.

All suits relating to Chagrin Falls take place in Bedford Municipal Court, the court in which the judge (Peter Junkin) about whom I wrote an editorial presided. Bedford had two judges. The other one was Junkin's law partner when they had a private practice prior to becoming co-judges in Bedford. His name is Brian Melling. I felt I was reading an "Archie" comic book. Do these guys do everything together?

In response to my suit for fraud, the condo hired a tall and cadaverous attorney to claim I was in default on a condo assessment. Condominium assessments are for capital improvements like new windows, etc. and all residents were allowed to pay for the most recent assessment in monthly installments for two years. I participated in this option and was current on my payments. The attorney filed an action in Bedford Municipal court for a judgment against me to find that I hadn't paid the assessment.

A court hearing was set.

I didn't understand this at all. I was current on the payments and all residents who paid on a monthly basis had a written installment agreement signed by all parties. It wasn't an obscure arrangement.

As it turned out, the condo attorney was on local boards and planning commissions. He acted as a mediator for a county court and had been practicing in the area for decades. His law firm was established in the area. I was learning a new lesson. You are not a "person" if you are not part of preferred relationships. Legal rights are administered on a tiered basis.

A magistrate presided over the hearing. She asked my response to the condominium Complaint which didn't mention the installment contract for the assessment. I admitted I owed money and described the installment contract. I said that although there was a balance due, the periodic payments under the contract were current and the contract expire on its own terms after 12 more payments. I didn't understand how an attorney who was so prominent and trusted would come in to court on the basis of a lie. How could he file a Complaint which disregarded a contract and a payment history on that contract which was a complete defense to his filing?

As I was to learn, this is a common tactic among attorneys all over the U.S. For someone naive, like me, the legal system is a standard of conscience and behavior that allows us to work as a group on a local, state and national level. You approach it in conformity with that standard and act on your obligation to acknowledge everything in favor of your adversary. A completely delusional stance.

Condo attorney saw the legal system as a limit on the extent to which you can lie, withhold essential information, deceive and distort. This is a fuzzy limit and its application has many variables, which include the competence of a judge, the familiarity of an attorney with a judge, the honesty of a judge, the political independence of a local judiciary and the amount of institutionalized corruption in a location. In some places, like Bedford, a preferred attorney is not subject to any limits.

The magistrate found that the entire amount of the assessment was due. This disregarded a year's worth of payments made prior to the hearing. It also disregarded the terms of the installment contract. A judgment for $2,600.00 was awarded against me, even though I had already paid almost half of the installments.

I stood there like a torn paper bag. Opposing counsel was remorseless. He and others like him had established a standard of legal practice in the area.

New Court

Once a judgment related to real estate is entered, a party can foreclose on the real estate to satisfy the judgment. A foreclosure action forces sale of the property and the proceeds go to the party with the judgment. Foreclosures are handled in another court. Since the amount of judgment was excessive and contrary to law,

I felt the foreclosure court would see that I had been paying on an installment contract and was current. It would see that the Bedford court made a "mistake".

It did. We had a marvelous magistrate name Amy Cuthbert who understood the defects of the prior court and made a proportionate ruling. Unfortunately, due to my inexperience, I was forced to pay attorney fees of $4,000.00. The Ohio foreclosure statute gives attorney fees to the foreclosing party. I paid the attorney fees according to the court instructions.

The foreclosure case was dismissed, with prejudice. We were now ready for the next round of financial fraud.

You Can Really Lie A Lot

Contentious financial relations with my condo continued. Opposing counsel filed a new suit in Bedford Municipal Court for a new judgment, in which, among other claims, he asked for unpaid attorney fees for the prior foreclosure action. I blinked at the document. You can't lie like THIS . . . can you? I mean, this was impossible. The docket of an entirely different court said I paid. It's on the record. At law "a court speaks through its journal". The docket is the court record of journalized activity. When a court record shows that a judgment is satisfied, it is law and can't be re-litigated. This is the application of *res judicata* and collateral *estoppel*.

I immediately filed a counterclaim for over $24,000.00 which was over the jurisdictional amount for Bedford Municipal Court. The assigned judge was Brian Melling, who the reader will remember was the law partner and co-judge with Peter Junkin, about whom I wrote the editorial.

Bedford is a municipal court with limited jurisdiction. One of its jurisdictional limitations is the dollar amount for cases it can hear. Ohio municipal courts can only hear damage claims up to $15,000.00. Fifteen thousand. This is limited by statute. ORC 1907.03 and Ohio Civ. Rule 13 J insist that a municipal court transfer a case beyond its dollar jurisdiction to the next court higher, which is Cuyahoga County Court of Common Pleas. There was no ambiguity. Jurisdiction is fundamental and anything a court does without Subject Matter Jurisdiction is a nullity and has no effect, ever. Absence of Subject Matter Jurisdiction can be challenged at any time, even for the first time on appeal, because an order entered without Subject Matter Jurisdiction never had a legal existence.

So, in response, J. Brian Melling gave me 30 days to pay the transfer fee or he wouldn't relinquish jurisdiction. He couldn't do this. There is no deadline to pay a transfer fee. In addition, since Melling didn't have jurisdiction, he couldn't make any rulings on the case other than to dismiss it and facilitate transfer to Common Pleas. In addition, I was out-of-state at the time trying to force my my mother's Trustee to relinquish the money he took from my mother's trust and didn't get Melling's order until after his illegal deadline had passed.

I rushed to send in my transfer fee a week late. Melling wouldn't accept it and reclaimed the case. I filed a Motion to Reconsider, reminding him he had no jurisdiction and could do nothing with the case. It was granted. Opposing counsel made a Motion to Reconsider and have the case reinstated in Bedford. It was granted. I made a Rule 60 motion telling the court that it had no Subject Matter Jurisdiction and told him how statutory authority left no room for ambiguous behavior. It was granted. Opposing counsel made a "Motion to Reinstate Case Nunc Pro Tunc (?) to have the prior order in my favor stricken and the case retained by Bedford. I waited for Melling's 4th order pertinent to this exchange

Melling should have been in a bind. In a decent court system, there would have been no uncertainty or motion practice around this issue. The case would have been set aside and transferred. But this was Cleveland where the practice of law and judicial behavior is completely personalized and unsupervised. What to do? How can you break the most fundamental laws of jurisdiction without getting caught? The answer is just don't worry about getting caught. No one cares about legal practice. Judges only have to worry about the police power and they control it. No one would obey the law if it wasn't enforced by the what is assumed to be the legitimate use of force by the police. Legitimacy comes from court orders referenced to a conscientious and accurate legal analysis. This nexus became undone in Cleveland. The practice of law in Cleveland became little more than judges exercising the police power on behalf of their friends and significant associates. They just bypassed the law.

Just Forge the Complaint

Melling's solution was to change my Complaint/Counterclaim. He reduced my claim from over $24,000.00 to exactly $15,000.00 to make sure he could retain the case and inflict damage on me. Now, this is criminal. The Complaint is unequivocally controlled by the Plaintiff. A judge may not edit or alter a Complaint or claim. He can only analyze it. Most judges are delighted to reduce their case load. Melling was doing everything he could to exercise a vendetta.

Nine months later, the court held a hearing of which I was not given notice. Since I wasn't there, opposing counsel got everything he wanted by way of Default

Judgment. Clerks of Court can be very useful. Although the Bedford clerk, Tom Day, had been indicted in 1986 and was named in a current indictment against County Commissioner DiMora as a party responsible for placing the women who provided DiMora with sexual services in municipal jobs, he retained his position and could determine who got notice. The court also neglected to send a copy of its order so I had no notice of its actions and couldn't file a timely appeal . . . which I couldn't have anyway since I was "vexatious litigator" and de facto banned from Ohio courts.

I requested a copy of the order and saw that J. Melling awarded opposing counsel the $4,000.00 in attorney fees which were already paid. Melling was on notice that this was a double payment. It was listed as an affirmative defense in my Claim/Counterclaim which Melling fraudulently altered.

When a judgment is paid, an attorney is obligated to file a Satisfaction of Judgment in the court from which the judgment originated. The Satisfaction had been due in Bedford within weeks of the time the foreclosure action was dismissed. I made a motion to have opposing counsel file the Satisfaction of Judgment and provided the canceled check and proof of payment from the court docket into which it was paid. I also proved the foreclosure was dismissed with prejudice after all amounts were paid. It was a matter of public record.

Opposing counsel wrote a response in which he told the judge to disregard the proof of payment and the docket record. Melling said O.K. He drafted an order which said opposing counsel didn't have to file a Satisfaction of Judgment. It contained no legal authority or analysis. There was no recitation of facts. Melling said "someone says the proper amounts weren't paid".

I made a timely motion to Set Aside Default Judgment. The American legal system doesn't like default and prefers to hear cases on the merits. It is usually very easy to have a default judgment set aside, especially if there are jurisdictional issues or claims that notices of hearing weren't received by a party. It was denied.

I filed a Writ of Prohibition in the local 8th District Court of Appeal. This writ is designed to prevent against the application of an order entered without jurisdiction and is not subject to a deadline. Since I was determined to be "vexatious" I had to ask "leave to proceed" from the 8th District. It was denied, without comment or explanation.

I tried the same writ in the Ohio Supreme Court which also has original jurisdiction to hear writs. It also denied permission to file.

14

Interlude
The Brutal History of Brenda Martinez

Debt is political memory.
No proud black woman should worry about Due Process

Brenda Martinez worked in the Cuyahoga County Recorder's office for seven years. She was hired by Pat O'Malley and conducted a happy and successful career during her 6 1/2 years with him. She was never disciplined and was promoted to supervisor. In late 2007 O'Malley left the office and a judge named Lillian Devezin Greene was named interim County Recorder. Lillian is the subject of Chapter 3 in this book.

Within months, Brenda was terminated by the interim Recorder for exercising her First Amendment rights. Brenda didn't exercise her freedom of speech in an aggressive challenge against her bosses or as to criticize policy. She was fired for repeating a joke she heard on the radio, in private, to another employee. Brenda was ruined because an interim executive with a narcissistic disorder and a diminished intellect couldn't control her temper.

I made it a point to interview Brenda.

Please tell me your connection to Cuyahoga County. Were you born here?

Brenda: I was born in Cleveland, Ohio. Cleveland proper.

Is Martinez your married name? What was your maiden name?

Yes. I married a Mexican and had three children with him. My maiden name was Zimmerman.

Did you go to school around here?

Yes. Lincoln West. My father worked for The Great Lakes as a supervisor in charge of tug boats and dredges. He worked right in Lake Erie.

When did you start working at the County?

August 2001. Before that I worked for Charter One Bank as an assistant bank manager and floated from branch to branch. I applied to the county because we were understaffed and overworked at the bank. There were also a lot of robberies. I just missed two that happened within a month. Floating worked. I wasn't at the particular branches when they were robbed.

Where did you work at the county? Who hired you there?

I worked at the County Recorder's office. Pat O'Malley hired me and started me in Public Information. He hired me to be a cashier but put me in a department that assisted walk-in and title representatives to get documents they needed. I was moved to Cashier in October of 2001. I was promoted to Cashier Supervisor in June 2006.

What skills do you need to be a supervisor? How big was your staff?

Knowledge of forms, the Ohio Revised Code, people skills to deal with the public and my staff. I supervised 8 cashiers of all races.

Were there any changes in the administration while you were there? I guess an Ex-Judge took over the Recorder's Office.

Yes. Pat O'Malley resigned in late 2007 and an ex-judge named Lillian Greene was named an interim director until the 2008 election.

What was Lillian like? How many people worked in the department? Did she have any experience with large offices?

She was so over her head. About 105 people worked in the Recorder's Office. Greene didn't have any experience with large offices. She was a judge with a staff of 2-3 people. No one was really introduced to her until she called a mandatory meeting for the entire office. Everyone had to be there early. She sent a letter saying everyone had to be there and people who didn't attend would be disciplined.

What went on in the meeting?

She said, "I'm Lillian Greene, the new recorder, not Patrick O'Malley. If you'd like to go work for him, I'll gladly take a resignation. She said she's tired of hearing Pat's name around the office and if anyone is caught saying his name, they'll be terminated. She said it's her understanding that Pat was outside the building talking with employees and she found this disrespectful. Someone told her Pat was outside the building a couple days earlier. She said if anyone was recording, she didn't care. That was it. She just basically threatened us. There was nothing nice or to encourage us to come to her with concerns or helpful ideas.

What was it like to work for her? Was anything different?

Nothing really changed. She didn't know anything about the Recorder's office, but we were all anxious about who might be fired in a new administration. The atmosphere changed because Pat was nice and we felt Lillian needed to keep us scared. Pat used to come around and say hello to everyone. Pat was liked. Lillian wasn't. She never made eye contact when she walked through the office and never spoke or said hello to anyone. Everything pretty much stayed the same, but it was more tense. She was so over her head in that position.

How long did you work there? Why were you terminated?

I was there 7 1/2 years. Lillian terminated me November 8, 2008 for telling a joke. I repeated a joke I heard on the radio. It was a friendly office. All the employees got along and we had been discussing politics and joking with one another for the months prior to the big election on Nov. 4, 2008. I was the only Republican and there was a lot of banter. It was all friendly. My department had two African Americans, five white people and a Hispanic. We used to make all kinds of jokes. Ethnicity didn't matter. We'd make Blonde jokes, Polish joke and jokes about all races. It was friendly. I voted for McCain. Obama won and the day after the election we were still chiding one another. People were making jokes to me like, "You can't have your bank bag because you didn't vote for Obama". One woman shut her door and put a "No Republicans Allowed" sign on it. It was funny. She did it because she knew me. An employee of Arab descent said he was glad McCain didn't win because he hated Palin and if I ever visited my son who was serving the Armed Forces in Alaska, I should visit Palin and learn how to hunt moose. Stuff like that. It was all friendly. I was listening to Obama stuff for an hour and a half including remarks like Obama's going to stop the damn Mexicans from coming across the border. My former husband is Mexican. I have three children who are half Mexican. Since the exchange became racial, I decided to respond in kind.

I told them I was glad Obama won, I was sure he'd do a fine job and I hoped he got Colin Powell as Defense Secretary. I left the group and walked to a desk 40 feet from the public reception counter where a security guard named Jerome Petro was sitting. Another colleague named Ron Mack was standing next to the desk. I repeated the following joke;

"They think one black man is going to run the white house, when it takes 11 to run a White Castle".

Everyone laughed and I went to lunch.

When I got back a woman named Mary Walsh, who I guess was with Human Resources of the Recorder's office, told me Mrs. Greene wanted to talk to me.

I went to Lillian's office. Lillian, Walsh and a woman who was Lillian's bailiff named Doreasa Mack were there. Greene didn't say hello, didn't ask me to sit down. She was standing there with an envelope in her hand and started screaming "Are you making racial comments?" I said "no". She asked, "Did you say anything about blacks". I said "No Ma'm. I have black family members (nephews, niece and a granddaughter) She started screaming, "I don't care. Are you calling Jerome and Ron a liar?"

Without giving me a chance to reply, she screamed, "Did you say White Castle?"

I said "yes".

She said, "You're terminated. Return your badge and get out of my office."

I didn't have my badge so Mary walked to my area. I handed her my badge and packed my belongings. I was horrified. I couldn't believe what happened. A black woman named Alnita who was one of my cashiers came over and said "I'm sorry, Brenda". Apparently everyone already knew because Greene was discussing this with staff members while I was at lunch.

I went home and cried for three days. I couldn't see. How can I feed my kids and mother? My mother lived with me. I called all three of the County Commissioners to defend myself and see if they would talk to Greene. The Commissioners never called me back. They're in charge of Greene and have to supervise her. They appointed her."

What about your property rights in your job? You were a state employee and were entitled to a legal procedure known as "Loudermill" rights, right. (See "Cleveland Board of Education v Loudermill" 470 U.S. 532 (1985)).

"I was a state employee and entitled to "Loudermill" rights. That means I should have gotten a formal letter with charges, notice of hearing, time to prepare for the hearing and an opportunity to have an attorney and witnesses at the hearing. It shouldn't have happened within 1/2 hour after lunch. She was a judge. Judges are supposed to follow the law and be fair. She was screaming like a wild pig. Also, what about free speech? Can't I talk about Pat O'Malley if I want? What about freedom of association? Can't employees meet with Pat O'Malley outside of work if they want? People like Greene can't be judges."

There you are, unemployed. Then what?

"I filed by myself with the State Personnel Board of Review. As a state employee I had a property right in my job. The SPBR could force the state to give me my job back. I also consulted with an attorney to see how I could get my job back. I decided to hire this attorney.

Things were going really well at the SPBR. They sent a copy of a letter sent to Greene asking for proof that she gave me my "Loudermill" rights. When Greene couldn't provide proof, the Hearing Officer (Lumpe) issued an order to Show Cause why this case shouldn't be decided in my favor and my job returned. I was going to win.

Everything would have gone well if I didn't hire a lawyer. My attorney filed an action in Federal Court to claim "Loudermill" rights. It was a disaster. You never file in Federal Court when you are in state court. I later learned that Federal Courts "abstain" or won't hear a case when a state proceeding is taking place. My attorney never should have filed in Federal Court. When the SPBR heard that a federal filing took place, it stopped all activity, took back its Order to Show Cause and gave all responsibility for the case to the Federal Court. That was also a mistake. The SPBR had no right to relinquish my case. It had to hear it since it was filed there first. No one knew what they were doing.

What should have happened, if the hearing officer, Federal judge and my attorney knew what they were doing, was the Federal Court should have refused to hear the case because it was in state court already and the state administrative hearing should have gone forward with the Show Cause hearing which would have given me my job back. Everyone failed. My attorney never should have filed, the Federal judge (Kathleen O'Malley) never should have heard the case and the SPBR never should have let the case out of its hands. Everyone failed.

But since we were in Federal Court, I had to follow the judge's decision. O'Malley ruled against me. Just a disaster. O'Malley said I was given "notice" under Loudermill by a note a coworker slipped me on my way up to Greene's office where I was fired. The note said "Lillian's pissed". That's notice of hearing? That gives me time to get an attorney, witnesses and organize evidence for a presentation? I heard Kate O'Malley got promoted or appointed to a higher position as a Federal Appellate judge. Why?

My attorney filed with the SPBR again on the merits. We lost. I appealed that decision in the SPBR. We lost. I appealed to Common Pleas and got judge Dan Gaul where we lost and made a final appeal in the 8th district, where Judge

Gallagher wrote the opinion in which I lost. It didn't make sense. It wasn't fair in terms of procedure or principle. It seemed like the judges didn't care about me or they didn't want to expose the failures of a local judge.

Had I done nothing other than file in the SPBR, I would have had my job back within 3 months. Instead, I had to pay an incompetent attorney to create risks I didn't need by filing in Federal Court when he knew I was about to win in SPBR. My attorney filed in Federal Court AFTER the SPBR issued its Show Cause order. Why would he do that? To make more money for extra filing? I was going to win. I was happy and was sure I was going to get my job back. Instead, I lost and had to pay legal fees."

What happened in the office after you were fired? Did Greene get people to falsify evidence to support her side of things?

"Yes. People started making up stories that they heard an African American customer complained about my joke. Impossible, because I whispered the joke to people 40 feet from the customer counter. It wasn't wrongdoing anyway. There's nothing wrong with repeating a joke I heard on the radio.

Then, at the SPBR hearing on the merits, Jerome Petro claimed he heard me say another joke that the White House would now be called The Black House. I never said this and it didn't make a difference anyway. People can make jokes and speak."

You never had any disciplinary record? Do you know of any other people accused of racist behavior in the county? What happened to them?

"No. Nothing. No discipline against me, ever. There was a girl named Genevieve Mitchell accused of treating white customers badly. A customer complained about her after his third episode of what he felt was racial hostility. She worked in the Public Information section of the County Recorder. She was called to the front office by the Chief of Staff (an Arab) who gave her a talking-to. Genevieve in turn wrote a letter to the Chief of Staff which they thought showed emotional problems.

Genevieve wasn't fired. She was sent to counseling. That's what you do. You help people a little bit. Everyone makes mistakes. Racism is part of life. Everybody's a little racist. You don't ruin someone's life for small statements that don't hurt anybody."

What was the date of your termination? How have you managed financially since then?

"I was fired November 8, 2008. I managed for a long time with the help of my Mom and fiance. Food stamps helped."

What about unemployment? Weren't you entitled to benefits? The state didn't try to deny these to you, did they?

"I applied immediately and was denied. Lillian Greene fought my application and told the commissioners who award benefits that I was a racist. Lillian wanted to make me suffer. She didn't pay the benefits. They don't come from her bank account. I didn't understand the commissioner decisions. They said that "I violated the policy and procedures manual". They said it violated . . . I don't know . . . a provision against aggressive language. I can't remember clearly. It doesn't matter. If the state didn't give me Due Process, we don't even get to the rules. You don't fire someone like Greene did. She's a judge?

I tried the unemployment board for benefits three times and lost. I then requested an in-person hearing. You can only apply three times. After the third denial, you can request an in-person hearing. I got my hearing and do believe it was for January 20, 2009. My attorney had federal court that day and faxed my file to the Unemployment Compensation Board of Review who in turn, told my attorney he was supposed to have called to say he couldn't make it and should have asked for a continuance. Faxing material wasn't procedure.

My hearing was dismissed and my claim denied. Thanks again to my attorney. So now we had to appeal the UCB ruling in Common Pleas, just to force a hearing. I want to say, in June of 2010, Judge Joan Synenberg, reversed and ordered my hearing. So, I had my hearing sometime in August by phone in my attorney's office. It was a two day process. They interviewed former colleagues from the Recorder's Office on the first day and then Lillian Greene and another man on the second. I was interviewed last. There was a lot of contradictory testimony on the Recorder's part and Synenberg noticed it. She also ruled that my attorney's conduct and fax was sufficient presence to hold a hearing. I got the case sent back to the state Unemployment Board.

When I got the Order from Synenberg granting my petition, I started crying. Finally someone saw me. Before she got the case, 5 judges and 2 administrative hearing offices kept making sure I could be fired without Due Process and denied unemployment benefits. I couldn't believe Lillian Greene was a judge. How could it be this difficult? Can't judges agree about something so easy to see? Why was Joan Synenberg the exception to bad judges and hearing officers?

I got lucky again. At the Unemployment Hearing, the officer started asking questions to see if Greene gave me my "Loudermill" rights. He wanted to know if

I got a formal letter describing my offenses. Greene said "no". He asked Greene if I had the opportunity to have a witness on my behalf. Greene said, "no". He then said . . . "and you fired Ms. Martinez why?" and Greene said, "because she told a joke about the president who is black and I am black."

I was interviewed last and told my whole story. In late September I received a letter from the UCRB and they said I was wrongfully terminated. They said I was not given Due Process or my Loudermill rights and while the joke was inappropriate, they did not find it to be racist nor did they feel it was a terminable offense.

They ruled in my favor. I got money October starting 2010, 2 years after my termination. It's over now. I used up the benefits. They aren't permanent."

How much do judges make? What about the pension for a judge?

"Oh God; judges make over 100k. Her pension must be close to 100K. Judges pay into PERS instead of social security. In addition, Greene was working as County Recorder WHILE she was getting a pension as a former judge. The County Recorder job paid about $75K or something like that. She was making close to $175K per year when she fired me and worked hard to make sure I couldn't work again or get unemployment benefits. Do you know what happens to your reputation in the state when you are fired? You're finished."

Have you been able to find any decent work in the past several years?

"No, and my mom died."

Sounds like you were subject to a vicious vendetta by Lillian Greene, completely disproportionate to the findings of the State Unemployment Compensation Review Board.

"Yup; along with J. Synenberg, they are the only ones who got it. It shouldn't be that difficult. I thought J. Gaul would be a good one, but he just went right along with Greene."

Any more difficulties?

"Well, my house was forced into foreclosure and I had to move in with my fiance. I'm still looking for a job. I have to put "fired" on my job application. I've had only 2 interviews in the past year and a half. No one called back. I've probably sent out 80 applications in the past 2 years."

Where's Lillian Greene, now?

"She's a visiting judge at Common Pleas. The Recorder's office was terminated under Issue 6. She lost her job when they changed the structure of county government. She actually sued the county for the balance of her contract and it was denied. She expected the county to pay her legal fees."

I saw that TV station WOIO did a piece on your termination and interviewed Greene. Did that help?

"No. No one cares about my story. I wrote the President of the US, McCain, Dennis Kucinich and Oprah. Obama's office sent me information on how to prevent foreclosure on my house. No one cares about the type of people we have here running the county. I offered to take a polygraph test on Oprah. I would LOVE for someone to give me a polygraph. Love, love, love.

It's bad that things go on like this. I loved my job, the customers and my co-workers. I'm not a racist. It's terrible that's what Greene labeled me. I stay in touch with my African American customers and co-workers. Some of them even wrote letters of recommendation for my various hearings. We're still in touch. This basically happened because of Greene's bad temper. I hope and pray to God I can get back in the work force.

Greene makes $175K per year and I have to worry about my mortgage. It wasn't enough for her to have everything. I had to have nothing."

15

In Seattle You Can Steal
from Unconscious Widows

Wolf's Gallery of Cleveland wasn't the only entity stealing from my mother. I had to protect her from my own family. While the corrupt legal administration of Cleveland was chasing me across the Eastern portion of the US, I discovered my mother's Trustee had secretly removed $94,000.00 from her trust and invested it in his own business. There was also another $20,000.00 taken for "miscellaneous" expenses.

The Trustee is a businessman in Seattle, Washington. His manner is severe, secretive and unsentimental. People always interpret this to mean "methodical and trustworthy", but what it really means is "removed and selfish". From prior conversations, I was sure he was autistic. I know him well, he is a family member.

We were put on notice of his sociopathic inclinations at his wedding 20 years earlier. My family had flown in from four different states to attend. The day before the ceremony, he announced that he failed to hire a caterer. I put myself through law school as a chef and felt it was natural to help. My sisters and I worked two days to provide food for 140 people after which was scheduled an intimate post-wedding party to which none of his family was invited. He even excluded his mother and father. We were expected to vacate his home so we wouldn't distract from this second event. But, on the basis of some projected virtues, he was named Executor/Trustee of two estates. They were my Aunt's estate and my mother's trust.

We weren't ready as a family to absorb or make the necessary conclusions from a series of events involving the Trustee and his fiduciary behaviors. The idea of financial misdeeds by a family member was unthinkable . . . from your mother was inviting damnation . . . and from 11 members of your family extending over three generations was bad risk management. The exposure was too large.

Plus, we were all Jews, right? We don't take from one another. Our "International Conspiracy to Control World Finance, Steal Funds and Violate Blonde N. Europeans" was directed against the goyim, not ourselves . . . right? Well, actually not. The Trustee ended up being able to charge for the time it took him to appropriate assets.

My father was an evolved and distinguished academic. He had a law degree from George Washington where he was Order of the Coif and a PhD in Public Administration. He was made to be a federal judge but chose to teach law and management He also acted as a consultant on an international basis for large private and public corporations.

We were raised in the humanist milieu of a central European scholar. Humans weren't objects of theft. They were things to be enlarged and developed. Money wasn't the object of life, realization of talent and an individual's internal world were priorities. Become what you are and the money will follow. We weren't wealthy, but the elegance of my father's life imparted things money couldn't buy. My father managed to maintain a household of innocence, competence and beauty. After his death, we became unprotected and subject to predatory intent.

My father departed in August of 2000. His sister, Anne followed one month later. The loss of my father removed a portion of the Earth for my family. He lived in a state of grace and displayed the generosity of someone who felt the abundance of his own talents. He was a one man civilization and his life illuminated and enlarged all those with whom he had contact. After his death, I operated in a significantly diminished capacity for a year. His sister's demise was too soon after his and exaggerated the pain of his departure from the world. It forced us to re-experience his loss.

My aunt had a substantial estate accumulated over 60 years of working for the Library of Congress in Washington, DC. It was left to nine beneficiaries and was described in a simple will. There was no real estate to sell and no disputes about how to interpret the will. Washington, DC has a statute which allows an Executor to proceed without the supervision of an attorney. Wills of this nature take four to six months to distribute and close.

After one and a half years, my aunt's estate had not been distributed. Her bank accounts had not been put in a special fiduciary account and no information was given to the beneficiaries about the size of her estate or anything else. In response to my questions about why this was taking so long, the Executor would say he was still discovering assets. There was no discovery to make. The estate consisted of cash accounts and some other liquid financial documents to disburse.

I called several estate attorneys in Washington, DC and Virginia. Most of them screamed at me to get the Executor out of the estate. He had misappropriated funds and was not complying with his accounting duties. They all agreed that the estate should have been closed a year earlier. I hired an attorney named John Dunn, who forced an accounting and disbursement. It was expensive and left a lasting anger.

I conducted all the investigations and paid all the attorney fees myself. None of the beneficiaries acknowledged my help or offered to contribute to the attorney fees.

Fiduciary Theft II
It's So Easy to Steal from An Elderly Widow When She's Unconscious

My aunt's estate was just the first example of an Executor/Trustee's misappropriation. After my father's departure, my mother moved to Seattle. It was a mistake. She was stricken by the loss of her husband and was excited by the novelty of a new location, but failed to acknowledge her dependence on the mercantile instincts of her son who didn't invite her into his own house, but allowed her to live at one of his assisted living facilities . . . as a paying resident. Within a month, she became isolated and lonely.

My mother didn't need a place. The house in Cleveland was paid off and her pension was more than adequate. She needed company and a daily social structure, which she had in Ohio. Her house was sold and the proceeds directed to a Trustee in Seattle, the same relative who administered my aunt's estate.

The Trustee had control of my mother's entire life. He had what is known as the Trifecta: Trustee for her Living Trust, Power of Attorney for her affairs and appointment as Guardian as she became incompetent. This status existed for the seven years between the demise of my father and my mother's departure.

A Washington state Trustee must provide annual accountings for the trust. The Trustee wouldn't provide them.

A Washington state Trustee is not permitted to make investments without court permission. The Trustee secretly took $94,000.00 and invested it with Morris Piha of Seattle.

A Washington state Trustee is not allowed to invest in his own business. Self-dealing is a huge violation. The Trustee was a partner in the Morris Piha Real Estate Trust. He was investing in his own business.

Estate disputes are litigated in the *Ex Parte* division of the King County Washington Superior Court. There is a special process called TEDRA which is designed to facilitate and accelerate the resolution of trust disputes. The *Ex Parte* division is run by commissioners who act as judges. Their rulings have force of law. King County Washington *Ex Parte* is known to be the most corrupt and partisan department in King County. You don't have to make reference to the law, you just have to be a local attorney on good terms with the commissioners and show up.

I was learning the hard way that possession is 10/10ths of the law. Litigation is very expensive and estate work is very complex. The financial documents are burdensome and a dishonest attorney knows how to avoid his obligation to be forthcoming by obscuring information. The burden of proof is still on the party claiming injury and in a Trust dispute in which the Trustee has withheld all information it's hard to prove anything.

Now there is a legal adjustment that happens when a fiduciary has violated his accounting duties. The burden of proof shifts to the fiduciary to prove that he has NOT committed wrongdoing. A presumption of wrongdoing is created against a trustee who has not provided statutory financial documents. But what happens in a TEDRA action is that there is a stay on all litigation while mandatory mediation takes place. A dishonest trustee is off the hook until mediation is finished. A skillful attorney can force mediation to take place over 3 years by asking for documents in a serial manner and redefining the scope of the mediation. Mediation is conducted by independent attorneys and firms which specialize in TEDRA matters. They have to be paid. I would also have to travel to Seattle for the sessions.

I called some attorneys in Seattle who specialized in Trust disputes. They wanted retainers between $20,000.00 and $50,000.00.

Most importantly, I was going broke. Defending against the Cleveland charges tapped my savings. In addition to bail payments and travel, I couldn't work. Fresh felony charges don't engender confidence in an employer and being absent for 3 days at a time, twice a month, makes an absentee problem. The Ohio prosecutors, Bill Mason, Tom Hanculak and Joe O'Malley knew exactly what they were doing. You don't just win a case; you ruin a person's life. The end-game is appropriating control over another person's destiny.

I was now excluded from professional life for exercising my First Amendment rights. The corrupt Cleveland legal system was determining events in Vermont and Washington state.

In a workable legal system, my mother's Trustee should have been terrified. In a partisan system, he was quite comfortable. His attorney had been in practice for over 50 years and knew all the judges and magistrates. As I mentioned above, the Ex Parte Probate division of King County Washington Superior Court is known as the most partisan division in the court system. It is common for attorneys to get anything they want from a Commissioner with whom they are on good terms. "Anything they want" means anything, however disproportionate or illegal.

Since the estate action was under a mediation order, I couldn't file additional motions pertinent to Trust financial matters and disbursement. However my mother was still subject to a Guardian who was stealing from her. I read through the Washington statutes and found one which described a procedure to have a Guardian removed. I called some attorneys in Washington State and the King County Clerk of Courts. They all said I could file to have the Guardian removed and could even use the existing TEDRA cause number if I wanted to avoid an additional filing fee.

I filed to have the Guardian replaced with a third party other than myself and cited the unauthorized theft of $94,000.00 from my mother's account, her diminished state from Alzheimer's and the mandatory accountings which had been missing for 4 years. I was sure the other side would rush to abdicate his status as Guardian. It didn't.

The Trustee's attorney claimed I violated the Meditation Stay and moved to have me sanctioned for $10,000.00. This was the shrill tactic of a loathsome and demented character. It was like a murderer charging a victim's estate for the time it took to kill him and the subsequent legal defense. I looked up Washington sanction law. Courts are allowed to award an attorney for the amount of time it takes to defend against a bad filing. Not only was my filing good, but it only took opposing counsel one half hour to protest the document

Any decent judge would see my filing was to protect a vulnerable geriatric. I did not claim money or damages for myself or anyone else. In addition, my filing was not related to the financial issues of the TEDRA action. Sanctions were unthinkable . . . until a diseased mind thought of them.

We had an indecent judge. Commissioner Watness immediately awarded $6,000.00 in sanctions against me. This was surreal. These things can't happen in America.

I immediately filed a Civ. Rule 60 motion to claim an error of law. Rule 60 motions are a form of appeal in the court of original jurisdiction prior to appeal in an appellate court and are filed in the court which made a ruling against which someone claims mistake or error of law. Washington sanction law is very clear, sanctions can only be awarded on a calculation of the time it took opposing counsel to prepare a response to a "frivolous" (whatever that means) document.

Opposing counsel immediately asked for another $10,000.00 in sanctions for filing a Rule 60 Motion. The commissioner gave him another $5,500.00. Again, there were no findings of fact or rulings of law which were necessary in a judge decision for sanctions.

I was being fined 1st degree Felony amounts by the party who was stealing from my mother. A court is supposed to protect geriatrics, not punish those who seek to defend them. The more I presented moral content to a court, the more viciously I was received. Commissioner Watness was confirming and enabling the mentalities which steal from their own mothers when they are in a diminished state. I was an outsider who was not part of the ethic of distribution in the local legal community.

This behavior on the part of the Commissioner and the Trustee's attorney should have been publicized outrage. It wasn't. The judge who heard the Rule 60 motion left the sanctions intact. There was no reference to conscience. There was no reference to law. There was no acknowledgment of duty towards a benevolent mother who needed her assets protected while she endured Alzheimer's disease. The judges and commissioners in Seattle were primarily concerned with maintaining their local relations at the expense of analysis.

Court Orders Don't Matter
You Can Charge for Time Spent Stealing

My mother departed in July of 2008 and it became time to close her Trust and finish the TEDRA filing. A TEDRA action concludes with what is known as the "Initial Hearing". It's a deceptive term because it is actually the last hearing, barring motions to reconsider and appeals, in the procedure. It is the hearing at which a final accounting is presented, approved and an order to disburse assets is made. The Trustee's attorney presented an accounting through 2006 which was missing 2 years and which also approached 600 pages. It was designed to avoid any reference to embezzlement, but the final figures were approximately what I projected them to be if the years between 2006 and 2008 were included. I decided to approve the accounting and flew to Seattle for the hearing.

The Commissioner made a simple order: 1) cash assets were to be disbursed within 10 days, 2) a small amount was reserved for taxes and was to be disbursed if no appeal of his order was filed in the state Appellate Court and 3) a real estate asset in the trust was to be divided and paid to 4 beneficiaries. The real estate asset was worth approximately $75,000.00.

No appeal was filed. The Trustee refused to divide the real estate asset and allowed his attorney to take additional fees from the amount reserved for taxes. These attorney fees weren't included in the Intial Hearing accounting, which already made a dispensation for attorney fees. That dispensation limited the amount of fees which could be paid to the attorney who represented the Trustee and the Trust. Trustee's attorney just took more in addition to those allowed and limited by law.

It's also noteworthy that the attorney who was defending a Trustee found to have embezzled from the Trust also was allowed access to the Trust, and act as if he was defending the Trust. This is a massive conflict of interest, which was raised to the Commissioner and disregarded. The people stealing from my mother were also in charge of her defense . . . and sanctioned in this regard by a court. The truth is much stupider than fiction.

The Trustee attorney's strategy was to inflict a cost against an aggrieved party to enforce any of his/her legitimate expectations. It's a foul and criminal mentality which a legal system should expose and punish. In Seattle *Ex Parte*, it was embraced, encouraged and enabled.

I insisted that Trustee attorney's and the Trustee partition the real estate as ordered by Commissioner Watness. Partition means "Meaningful Distribution of Legitimate Expectations", or the retention of an appraiser to ascertain the real estate's cash value and sale of the real estate or a buy-out by one of the joint tenants. In response, the attorney sent everyone a document that they owned a one quarter share. There was no cash distribution, no appraisal and no information about the amount of money this asset earned on an annual basis. There was no dialogue.

I made a motion to Commissioner Watness to enforce his order of partition. He refused and claimed he no longer had jurisdiction. This was a spectacular lie. All courts retain jurisdiction to enforce their own orders. Watness was making a career out of being a flaccid shill for the conditions he thought maintained his career. I called around and asked some local attorneys what to do. The consensus was an action in Partition. I read the statute and decided to file.

I could have also brought an action for contempt. Washington state has a statute which is addressed to the City attorney, who decides to bring it as a criminal action or not. I actually called the Seattle City Attorney, a man named Craig Simms and sent him all relevant court orders and a copy of the state contempt statute. Craig called and asked me for an interview. I flew out to Seattle and met with him. I also described how the statute had been construed in the past. A month after my return to Vermont, Simms sent a belated response in which he declined to bring contempt.

Partition is an action to divide real estate. It orders a party to do exactly what I had been asking from the Commissioner, the Trustee and his attorney. A successful action will order an appraisal, sale and proportionate disbursement of cash. I filed my Complaint in Partition and received Trustee attorney's motion to dismiss. It was denied by Commissioner Tinney. I made a motion to amend my complaint which was granted by the Commissioner. A case management schedule was created. This set out the times within which parties had to complete "discovery" and file dispositive motions which could terminate the action before trial. Trustee attorney refused to comply with discovery. He refused to answer my interrogatories (written questions) and refused to comply with my Requests for Production (requests for documents and other physical items). This is contemptuous behavior. I made a Motion to Compel Discovery, which was granted by a second Commissioner, who issued and Order to Compel. The history of the case was going against opposing counsel, rapidly. I was sure he'd capitulate.

Washington State's Secret Body of Law

A propos to nothing, Trustee's attorney made a Motion for Summary Judgment against me. These are heard by the Judge. Under certain circumstances, Commissioners act in an ancillary supportive role to a judge, but dispositive, large motions are heard by the Judge. The grounds for the Motion claimed that I cited an unpublished case. Washington State has an idiosyncratic rule which bars unpublished appellate cases from being used as precedent. Washington State has basically approved a body of secret law in which a court can avoid being told or held accountable for what it has done. Even in the appellate case didn't have precedential value under *Stare Decisis* (courts are bound to follow rulings of law on prior cases with the same fact circumstances) it still is evidence of legal analysis. The rule does NOT remove the precedential effect of rulings from Courts of First Resort and this case I cited was affirmed by the local appellate court. That means I had support in two courts for this case and didn't even have to rely on its presence in the Appellate court.

Considering how uncooperative opposing counsel had been with respect to discovery and all other matters, the amount of time he spent on the case was minimal. His Answer to my Complaint was two pages and his motions to dismiss were one half page each. Maybe he spent two hours total on the case.

In conjunction with his Motion for Summary Judgment, he asked for $11,000.00 in attorney fees. Hearing was set for March.

Judge Appel awarded Trustee's attorney Summary Judgment and all his attorney fees. It was a two sentence order with no findings of fact of rulings of law. J. Appel didn't know the file and admitted that "he never understood this case". Attorney fees are normally not awarded unless there is a contract or statute for their payment. They can also be paid for the time to defend against "frivolous" conduct, but J. Appel specifically found there was no "frivolous" conduct here. Even if "frivolous" conduct was found, opposing counsel only spent two to four hours on the case and was still in contempt of the Commissioner's Order to Compel.

There was no substance to J. Appel's order and fees cannot be charged without findings of fact and law. Finally, Summary Judgment is never granted prior to the end of discovery. It is a motion which states that there is no issue of fact and shouldn't be filed until all facts are accumulated during discovery. Just moving for Summary Judgment prior to the end of Discovery shows bad faith or real confidence that the judge can be reached.

There is another fundamental matter which Appel's order disregarded. That is the "American Rule". The "American Rule" of attorney fees is a presumption, barring contract or statutory provision that all parties pay for their own attorney fees. It is a very strong presumption which is difficult to undo . . . in a non-partisan legal forum.

I called some attorneys in Seattle to find out why the judges break the law. They said it's because the system is ruined. Judges have favorites and will protect their political allies. One also mentioned that J. Appel works in Snohomish Superior Court and "weird stuff happens there". She also said it's death to represent someone in a "foreign" jurisdiction, even one in a contiguous county like Snohomish is to King County.

My face was getting hammered for acting on the most legitimate expectations of what the American legal system represented itself to be.

I decided to try the local appellate court and filed an appeal.

You Don't Expect Us to READ This, Do You?

Trustee's attorney immediately filed what is called a "Motion on the Merits". This is an appellate motion designed to screen bad appeals at their inception. These appeals are ones which don't recite legal criteria, are factually impossible or which are filed after an identical appeal by the same filer had been previously heard and denied. The motion was denied. I won. This proved my case had merit. I submitted my brief and the case was assigned to J. Michael Spearman.

I looked him up. He had an unlikely profile. Michael Spearman was a 60ish African-American who went to Brown University and was a Union Representative for a time. I guess he was in manufacturing prior to law school. Union participants know one rule. Maintain and get income for your group. It's a brutal and effective ethic.

Spearman did not run for judge, but was appointed when a judge in the Appellate Court left officer prior to the expiration of his term. When that term was over, Spearman ran unopposed. It didn't seem unusual to me but was told this was a tactic used by political parties and interest groups to maintain a position. (In Washington, judge candidates are not overtly identified to political parties) A judge who knew he wasn't running for the following term would leave early giving his affiliates time to appoint his successor. I was also told beating an incumbent judge in an election was almost impossible.

J. Spearman brought judicial defect to new and unobserved territory. He wrote an order in which he said he would not consider my argument. He said he would not read my most fundamental presentation. Judges HAVE to read arguments, even if they are bad ones. He didn't even feel the need to be discreet.

He also awarded attorney fees for the appeal; even though I won the Motion on the Merits. So, the party who helped steal from my mother and who remained in contempt of a court order to partition real estate was now able to fine me at two levels of state court. J. Spearman upheld a lower court judgment for slightly over $11,000.00 in attorney fees and added an additional $3,500.00 for the appeal.

Had I accidentally filed in N. Korea? Was my case mistakenly placed on the docket of some Post-Stalinist kleptocracy run by a secret society organized during law school at "The People's Democratic School of Law and Correct Collectivist Acting"? Or maybe I just was opposing the attorney who had deep mob connections or naked pictures of every judge en flagrante with other species.

I called the Washington State Commission on Judicial Conduct. The representative agreed that a judge has to read arguments and that attorney fees seemed to be without legal basis. There was no contract or statute awarding them. She asked me to send in a written grievance. Three months later I received an enigmatic letter saying no misconduct had been found. There was no analysis or reference to the facts of my grievance.

The judicial failures were searing. Not only were no attorney fees forthcoming in the lower court, but they were criminally over-charged and fraudulently submitted. It must be remembered that opposing counsel wouldn't even participate in discovery and filed documents which took about four hours to prepare. In addition, he was in contempt of a court order to partition real estate and under an order to compel compliance with discovery in the Partition action. Plus, he and his client had already mis-appropriated tens of thousands from my mother on the basis of illegal accounting practices.

My only remedy, other than assassination or vivisection, was to the Washington Supreme Court, which grants discretionary appeal from the state Appellate Division. It's not automatic.

Washington state has enabled itself to hide judicial misconduct by hiding cases. It distinguishes between "Published" cases, which have precedential value, and "Unpublished" cases, which may be printed, but which do not have precedential value and which do not have the value of Stare Decisis in a subsequent case. In Washington state, publication is optional unless a court allows its activity to be used. In short, Washington has given itself the means to hide the illegal behavior of its judges. Under state and court rules, opinions must have precedential value to be published; see RCW 2.06.040 and RAP 12.3(d). This means that the judge who intentionally failed at the appellate level can deny a motion under RAP 12.3. to have his behavior exposed.

So, I had to ask the court to have my case published. J. Spearman's behavior and that of a prominent attorney, a real estate developer and a Commissioner in a lower court would remain unknown unless the case were published.

Predictably, the Appellate Court refused to allow publication.

The Washington Supreme Court refused review.

No one will ever know.

Where are my automatic weapons? Why hasn't anyone organized an assault on municipal court buildings? The people stealing from my mother managed to fine me close to $26,000.00 for their crimes. The parties embezzling from her while she was suffering from Alzheimer's were paid attorney fees from her Trust while being able to claim the presumption of virtue from the courts.

Did N. Korea establish a quiet lobby in Washington state? Maybe the guys in Iran know something about Americans. Maybe they really have something to say.

16

The Ohio Offense That Would Not Die

Pleeeease Bring me to Trial

I finally heard from my attorney. He called on a Sunday to say I should have been in Ohio last Thursday for a pre-trial. A warrant had been issued for my arrest. He didn't mention anything about the trial which didn't take place and was unapologetic. I fired him and notified the court. He wasn't concerned about being accountable to any person, institution or principle. The legal system had lost its super-ego. I looked into the dense, grey moisture of Vermont's early spring and contemplated what to do next . . . now that I was a fugitive . . . again.

I feverishly called the judge's office and explained that my attorney didn't tell me of the pre-trial. Surprisingly, Mary Pat agreed to recall the warrant and reschedule the pre-trial. This would be the 6th meeting in Ohio. Her manner had softened and she was even a little conciliatory. I also made a motion to have counsel appointed. I was getting down to my last $1,000.00.

A very affable person named Bob Tobik called. He was the head of the Cuyahoga County Public Defender's office. I explained the history of the case. He didn't seem alarmed by the circumstances. When I asked how the prosecutor could maintain a charge without jurisdiction and when it knew of my alibi defense, he made friendly noises without really telling me anything. I drove in for the pre-trial and walked over to the Justice Center with Bob. It was very odd to walk across Lakeside Blvd. as a felony defendant. My father used to cross this street on his way to be consulted by County executives for his expert opinions.

We went up to the 17th floor where a very familiar scene was repeated. I sat by myself while my attorney spoke with the prosecutor in a private room. After 10 minutes, Bob came back and asked me if I wanted to take a misdemeanor plea. I said of course not. I wasn't guilty of the charges. He went back to his conference and came back after 5 minutes. The prosecutor wouldn't drop the charges.

On the way back to Bob's office, I asked what could possibly have happened the day for which the trial was set. I also wanted to know if he could re-present all my defenses which included the Grand Jury "No Bill", the case of "Froehlich" which states that a "No Bill" terminate prosecution in favor of the accused, passage of the statute of limitations, absence of jurisdiction and the impossibility of doing the things of which I was accused.

The statute under which I was charged applies felony liability for people who alter the original of a court document. If I wasn't in Ohio, how could I have had access to an original court document? Original court documents are kept in the office of the court's clerk. There are two ways to get access to them. The first is by entering the clerk's locked and secured office and getting records. The second is to come in as a client and ask the clerk for a file with an original record. Depending on the office, they will allow you to have a file for inspection in their reception area. A party can then read that file while the clerk watches. The second way is by entry into the clerks' secured area. I was accused of altering a document from Lakewood Municipal court, which is a small court. The clerk's office is a very small space and has just a couple employees. Anyone without permission to be in the file area would be recognized and removed immediately. The police station is in the same building as the Lakewood Municipal court.

The offense of which I was charged was designed to punish court employees who use their position of advantage to alter original documents to which they have special access. This would include things like driver licenses which could be duplicated and sold to illegal drivers or court orders awarding money damages. If there was no alteration of an original court document or fraudulent alteration of a will to increase one's inheritance, then all other offenses under my statute were misdemeanors for which the statute of limitations had passed years ago.

I asked Bob why we just didn't do a Writ of Prohibition. This would have ordered the lower court to stop prosecution of a case for which it didn't have jurisdiction. Ohio had no Territorial Jurisdiction because nothing took place there at or near the time alleged. I was out of state. He grimaced and told me, "you don't want to start filing any writs or things like that. Just let me handle this". Given my circumstances, I thought he would welcome the involvement of a higher court. It seemed like every court in Ohio had to rule in our favor. I still wasn't getting it.

I drove back to Vermont and drafted several briefs reciting the reasons this case should be dismissed. Bob assigned the case to a very unpretentious and likable assistant named Chris Maher. I later discovered Chris was one righteous fucker who actually jumped on a police officer in Columbus, Ohio to protect a friend being beaten during an arrest. At times, I would find Chris sitting in the bus stop outside his office, having a cigarette. He'd be dressed in jeans and a hoodie. You'd never think he was an attorney at work.

Chris complimented me on my work. He found it original and useful. When I asked about the failed trial, he had no explanation. I also wanted to know why the court hadn't ruled on any of my motions. Chris said Cuyahoga County decides everything at trial. It's an "all or nothing" proposition. I recited the Ohio Rules for Superintendence of the Courts which insist that all motions be decided within 120 days. The court could dismiss this case if it wanted. So could the prosecutor who was obligated to acknowledge exculpatory evidence and jurisdictional defects. I called an attorney to find out why this case was still active.

Attorney: "You don't get it. You still think in terms of three outcomes; the judge dismisses the case before trial, the judge rules for you at trial or the judge rules against you at trial. There's another alternative . . . the judge does nothing."

Author: "A judge can't do that. He has to follow the rules."

Attorney: "No he doesn't. A judge will refuse to act at times. It's the 4th alternative. Even though you think he "has to". A judge can disregard rules. No one can force a judge to do anything, especially in Cleveland, which is the worst place in the country. Anyway, you still don't understand the interests being calculated by the parties. The judiciary is an interest group, just like the prosecutor and everyone else. The strange thing about your case is the people driving it. It adds a distorted influence to the way it's going.

"What interests?"

"There are 36 judges in Common Pleas. If ten-fifteen thousand people are indicted by the Grand Jury every year that's approximately 400 to 500 criminal cases assigned to each judge every year. Add on to that another four to five thousand pending cases from the prior year and you're looking at two criminal cases a day. There are like 26,000 cases pending in just the Asbestos docket.

The civil division gets 40 to 50 thousand new cases every year and drags another 20-30 thousand from the prior year. That's about 75,000 cases. After they are distributed, judges have about 1300 to 1500 civil cases assigned to them every year. Two criminal cases plus four to five civil cases per day makes six to seven cases per day a judge has to read. It's a lot. Too much, really. So, naturally, they want to edit cases. Deals get made.

Really good deals get made with attorneys they know.

Judges aren't all alike. Some are smart. Some are dumb. Some are fair. Some are biased. Some work hard and know their files. Others know very little about their cases and try to educate themselves about a case during trial. Some are heavily politicized and endorsed by Unions and the demographic groups here. You can't rely on anything. One thing that does matter is personal relations and favors.

"Judges can't do favors", I said.

"How did you ever reach adulthood? I can't believe you survived this long. Here's what's probably going on in your case. You pissed off some mad-dog judge from Bedford. The courts of Bedford are an organized criminal enterprise. You aren't allowed in there unless you are dirty. Someone powerful wants you dead and called McFaul (County Sheriff) to make sure you died. McFaul is filthy. He forces his own employees to make election contributions. Over one half of his deputies didn't take the Civil Service exam. The police are owned and will do whatever is necessary to remain living indoors. McFaul got his deputies, who no one else would hire to clean urinals, to lie to the Grand Jury. Someone also contacted Bill Mason, the prosecutor. When a judge wants a favor and his friends include the County Sheriff and prosecutor, he'll get whatever he wants.

Even if the judge assigned to your case likes you and thinks you are getting a raw deal, he'll acquiesce to an illegal agenda, in varying degrees, to maintain a working relation with the prosecutor. A prosecutor can force a judge to hear a lot of cases he may not want to hear and exhaust that judge. There's a tit for tat. If the judge refuses to dismiss a dirty case like yours in exchange for past and future dispensations from the prosecutor, the judge manages to stay current with his docket. He also maintains a friendly relation with the political machinery of the prosecutor which includes unions and other voting blocs.

If a judge allows the prosecutor to stress you and keep the case on his docket, which uses that judge's time, he'll expect the prosecutor to settle other cases without trial. The idea is to maintain the working relationship with the prosecutor and police.

It doesn't mean the judge is a bad guy or that he's against you. The judge in your case actually has an O.K. reputation and knows his files. It means he's caught in something larger than himself and runs the risk of losing his position if he can't keep up with his docket or maintain himself in the local political organizations. Bill Mason and the totality of circumstances create forced choice.

Welcome to the world of elected judges. In Ohio, judges are allowed to hear cases litigated by attorneys who donated to their campaigns. The judges keep lists of people who contributed. I think there is 1 Republican judge in Common Pleas. Judges are elected on the basis of party affiliation and the Democratic Party runs the county.

The public defender is also influenced by it. They'll yield to the prosecutor on certain small and unpublicized cases to get more important concessions from the judge and prosecutor on larger cases. Being known as a cooperative person can turn aggravated assault into disorderly conduct.

Meanwhile, everyone wants to win because it proves they are earning their salaries. Bill Mason will send people to jail for crimes they didn't commit just to claim he gets results. His conviction rate is so high because he hides evidence. Everyone is getting real sick of him, but no one can do anything about it. The idea is to control outcomes and Mason has spent a lifetime doing it. He controls the entire county.

Actually, from looking at your case, I think the judge likes you and wants the prosecutor to fuck off, but he won't. The judge can take your side on this one because you are small, alone and invisible. He can maintain a stance in your favor because the stakes are low

Grow up. I expected more from you. Jesus. Thank God your dad isn't around to see he gave birth to Bambi."

Oh. I didn't know.

Meanwhile… back to my existential matrix. Two more pre-trials were scheduled at which nothing was resolved. I still was not privy to the conversations which took place between my counsel and the Prosecutor even though the pre-trial schedule said they had to take place before the judge.

Trial was re-set for June of 2008. I drove in. No one arrested me this time. My attorney and I walked over to the Justice Center together. There was a short conference between him and the prosecutor, after which I was told the trial was canceled. The prosecutor would accept a plea, though.

I refused a plea but didn't go back to Vermont this time. I had to stay for abdominal surgery at the local University Hospitals.

Mother Departure

My mother departed shortly after my abdominal procedure. She was a benevolent and generous person. It was odd to sit with my family at the service in Cleveland. These were the same people who sat together in court against me in the real estate partition action. The malaise of public life found expression in my family life. The unthinkable had become conventional practice. The ethic of unilateral loyalty to family practiced by my parents became extinguished in one generation.

I couldn't tell them of my circumstances for fear they'd use them against me. The Trustee's attorney never failed to mention that I had been declared "vexatious" in Ohio during the Trust proceedings in Washington State. It didn't matter that I had been declared "vexatious" while defending my mother.

Two Days, Two Trials

I was now becoming concerned that the two offenses for which I was being charged would influence one another. Any sentencing in Common Pleas for the felony charges would be influenced and enlarged by the Bedford/Parma menacing/ telephonic harassment charges, if they were recorded as prior offenses. The reverse would also be true. The Parma court would regard any Common Pleas conviction as a prior offense for purposes of sentencing and impose a more severe sentence because of it. Bill Mason and Joe O'Malley really knew how to dispose of a human.

In the meantime, another trial was set for September 2008 in Common Pleas for the felony charges. I drove in from Vermont. It took two days because I was still recovering from surgery and kept falling asleep. My attorney and I met on the 17th floor of the Justice Center, where he attended a private meeting with the prosecutor. He came in to the conference room where I was adjusting my tie and preparing documents to tell me the trial was canceled, but they would take a plea today if I wanted. I refused. This was my 9th or 10th trip to Cleveland. Trial was re-set for the end of October, 2008.

Trial had also been set in Parma on the "menacing/telephonic harassment" charges two days before the Common Pleas felony trial.

During the interim, I drafted my trial briefs and consolidated all my defense briefs into one document. The prosecutors had no grounds to proceed on the basis of law or evidence. The Common Pleas judge refused to rule on my motions to dismiss and the Parma judge (J. Spanagel) refused to acknowledge the prior entry of "Not Guilty/Case Dismissed" in Bedford for the charges being re litigated in Parma. Since I couldn't get an attorney to touch my case, I had to go in alone.

Driving through the Adirondacks in fall is normally a pleasure. It had turned into an anxious tedium. The trip to Parma Municipal Court was my 10th or 11th trip by now. My savings were gone and I was living on the continental breakfasts at Shelly's North Star Motel. I was able to accumulate just enough every month to pay for gas.

I arrived pre-dawn and changed my clothes in a gas station. When I entered the court, I was met by a Detective Varza of the N. Royalton police department who shook my hand and informed me of a new charge against me; "Intimidation of a Witness". I wrote a letter to the witness who signed the "menacing" affidavit by which I explained it was illegal to sign a new affidavit for charges that had been dismissed with a finding of Not Guilty. The letter was business-like and direct. There were no threats and it was composed in the expectation that it would be shown to a court. A party always has the right to raise legal defenses and give a party notice that it has committed Abuse of Process. Varza used this letter as the basis for new charges.

Detective Varza didn't care about the law. He was part of an initiative to ruin the record against me. It didn't matter if I had done something illegal or not, he was instructed to provide the means for a court to enter convictions against me. There is a presumption of truth on a police criminal complaint. In Cleveland, the presumption is a device for the corrupt. Now I had a third charge.

The prosecutor, Joe O'Malley and I met in a quiet part of the court building. We didn't meet in front of the judges but had a settlement conference prior to trial. The judge was available and sitting at his bench for consultation. Joe asked if I wanted to take a plea for aggravated menacing and he'd drop some other charges. I said no. That's an offensive thing to have on a person's public history. I started to pack up when Joe told me that he wanted a conference with the judge. I stood in the shadowed corridor of Parma Municipal court waiting for Joe to return. He had a deal.

"Let's do this. We'll drop the intimidation of a witness and all other charges. I just cite you for a minor misdemeanor of "Disorderly Conduct". That's a minor misdemeanor and the lowest crime in Ohio. You'll be on unsupervised probation for two years. That means you won't have to report to a probation officer or anything."

I thought about it and realized it was the best thing to do. A minor misdemeanor is even lower than what I thought was the lowest Ohio misdemeanor, that of the 4th degree.

A plea gets me out of this with a scratch. It's a lie with which I could live. I said O.K. and Joe went back in the courtroom and returned with a paper. It was an agreement to dismiss the case. I signed it and went to my car. He didn't give me a copy.

The next day I called the court to see what Joe had given to the court. The clerk transferred the call to the Records department who looked in the file.

"You've plead to a conviction of Aggravated Menacing and Witness Intimidation. Sentence suspended, 2 years probation and forfeiture of bail. There's also a no-contact order. That means you can't contact the person who made the original criminal affidavit to the police."

I had been cheated again. I told her of our deal.

"No. That wasn't the arrangement. We agreed to "Disorderly Conduct" as a minor misdemeanor with all other charges dismissed.

"Sorry Mr. Grundstein, I can't change what's in the case notes."

Two days before my felony trial I was on record for Intimidating a Witness and Aggravated Menacing. I looked like a rabid sociopath. I'd also lost over $1200.00 in bail between the Bedford and Parma dispositions in this case and over $1000.00 in travel expenses.

Plea deals are agreements to accept lower charges in exchange for not making the prosecutor and court go to trial. That means a judge reading the file could guess that my originally charged offenses were significantly worse than the plea. Was there anyone who didn't lie in the Cleveland justice system? What would happen in Common Pleas two days later? I had to imagine the possibility that Joe O'Malley was in contact with the County prosecutor and would tell him of the entries against me. Or maybe the County Prosecutor would even call Joe in as a witness to testify about the Parma offenses

My attorney and I agreed to walk over to the Justice Center together on the day of trial. The hearing was set for 9:00. When we arrived at the 17th floor, we were joined by Bob Tobik, the Chief Public Defender, who was already there. That was nice. The head of the department was there for support. Bob and my attorney met with the prosecutor while I sat in a conference room. I had essentially done all the briefing and research for Bob's office during his involvement with the case. They all liked my work. Apparently I had provided case law and arguments about which they didn't know. I was adding to their inventory of significant knowledge.

Bob and Chris came back to the conference room where I was sitting. Bob spoke first;

"Hey Bob, the prosecutor has offered to let you go with a $50.00 (fifty dollar fine) if you take a plea. That's nothing; a slap on the wrist."

"To what would I be pleading?"

"They want to do misdemeanor falsification".

"What about my Bar status? Falsification is a crime of moral turpitude and the Bar's not going to like that. Too risky. I didn't falsify anything anyway. Everyone knows that."

Chris spoke next.

"Bob, you never know what's going to happen at trial. I'd hate to see you taken away in an orange suit."

I got scared. My own counsel was articulating the possibility of jail. This was also the first time they abandoned a stance against the prosecutor. If the judge had allowed the case to go this far under these circumstances, I had no reason to believe I'd get a fair trial. In addition, I had no right of appeal. Since I was declared "vexatious", the local appellate court could deny an appeal. None of the courts here had followed any rules or principles anyway. Even if I had a right of appeal, the courts would probably find a way to deny access to court or rule against me if I was able to exercise it.

"What about all my motions to dismiss? Why hasn't the judge ruled on them? Why should I have to go to trial when they have no jurisdictional basis for trial? I wasn't even in Cleveland at the time alleged. I sent him my alibi evidence. He has it. Why doesn't the judge see that?"

No one had a response. There were clucking noises and "tough break" sounds.

This had taken over a year and 11 trips to Ohio. My life had been stolen from me. I had no idea when this would end if I didn't take a plea and no idea what would happen in court if I went to trial. It seemed my own attorneys wanted to dispose of the case. Why would they encourage a plea when my evidence was decisive in my favor? I no longer trusted anything that went on here.

"What happens if I take the plea?"

"Well we go before the judge. The prosecutor will be there and the judge will ask some questions, like "Have you been offered anything to make this plea?" He'll also ask the prosecutor about prior offenses and his recommendations."

Oh, great. The prosecutor has the opportunity to bring up the Parma convictions. I no longer felt I could predict any future behaviors of any parties and decided to take the plea. I reasoned that a $50.00 fine would prove that any falsification was not serious, even though I was not in Ohio at the time of the alleged crime and I hadn't falsified anything as described by the indictment. I was being extorted into admitting something false about myself. Judges, police and prosecutors are supposed to protect the innocent. In Cleveland, they made a plan to punish an innocent party.

We all went in the courtroom. The judge was a smallish person with Mediterranean features and a slightly flattened nose. The prosecutor sat at the table next to ours. He was a young black man named Marcus. Bailiff Mary Pat Smith sat at a desk on the side. We all rose and the judge spoke.

"Well Mr. Grundstein, I suppose you want to get back to Vermont?"

My two counsel and I stood up to address the court. I spoke.

"Yes your honor. But I'd like ask why this case hasn't been dismissed. I'm sure this court knows of all my defenses"

"I've been told you've agreed to a plea. That is the scope of this hearing. What does the prosecutor have to say? Does he accept this plea? Are there any prior offenses of which he knows?"

I went black with anxiety. The three of us remained standing. It was a strangely noble file. We looked like a banc of military personnel standing against unjust charges.

"No your honor. There are no priors. We accept the plea."

It worked. The Parma clerk hadn't entered the Aggravated Menacing/Witness Intimidation convictions in their docket yet. There was nothing on the record and the Parma prosecutor, Joe O'Malley was not present as a witness. Maybe all the police, judges and prosecutors involved in the initiatives against me didn't know all the scheduled proceedings and events in both cases. I was still amazed no one called the Public Defender to tell him of the Parma proceedings.

The judge continued;

"Does Defense counsel have anything to say?'

Chris recited a lot of nice things about me and mentioned my surgery, the death of my mother and the quality of my work.

"He's been to hell and back, your honor. His Mom died. He had surgery. He's very intelligent and wasn't even in Ohio to commit an offense."

The judge addressed me.

"Has anyone offered you anything of value in exchange for your plea?"

"Yes your honor, they have agreed to dismiss the case with some misdemeanor charge and a Fifty dollar fine. This is my 10th or 11th trip to Cleveland and my fourth canceled trial. It's very valuable to avoid a felony and stop the trips to Cleveland."

"I wasn't referring to the plea agreement as something of value. Please sign the prepared paper and pay your $50.00 fine and costs to the criminal clerk on the second floor."

I was given a paper for the first time. It was a longish document and was signed by Detective Mackey and another sheriff's deputy. I had been careless and didn't ask my attorney exactly what the charge to which I was accepting a plea, said. I later discovered that it was not only an agreement to plead to a specific statutory provision, but also described specific behaviors I didn't commit and couldn't have committed because I wasn't in Ohio. The case was over. I couldn't keep driving to Ohio and I didn't trust any court to give me a fair trial. I signed and the judge tapped his gavel.

Fines are paid in the criminal clerk's office which is on the second floor of the building. I took the elevator down and went to the payment window where I wrote a check. One month later I received a letter from the Criminal Clerk asking me to pay my fine. I wrote back and said I had paid it and included the canceled check. More notices to pay were sent. I moved the court to notice payment on the record.

In 2011, three years later, the Chief Clerk Cuyahoga County Criminal Division, Mark Lime, was put in jail for embezzling fines, falsifying records and charging multiple amounts for the same offense. There were 76 counts.

19

Judge Nugent's Federal Property

Whoever was chasing me knew that I wasn't allowed to protect myself in state court. As a "vexatious litigator" I was also banned from all courts of first resort and couldn't file actions for Abuse of Process. I also couldn't file writs in the local appellate courts to stop serial actions for matters that had been dismissed or pursued without jurisdiction. Every time I asked for permission to file, it was denied, even though I never should have been declared "vexatious" in the first place. Entire institutions paid to prevent this sort of behavior agreed to make it happen.

So, I decided to file in Federal Court to enforce my right of access to the state courts of Ohio.

I was sure I'd find protection in the pristine and removed venue of Federal Court. After all, that's what federal court is meant to do; control the quality of state proceedings. A federal court would understand that I was sick of being the golf ball for the racketeers in charge of the Cuyahoga County legal system.

That turned out to be an optimistic lie. The federal system is meant to control the Constitutional quality of state courts, but it's designed so that the defects of the local state courts get imported into the federal ones. The federal courts become the means to insulate a corrupt state system from federal scrutiny.

Federal District courts are established on a regional, state basis. Ohio has two Northern Districts, East and West and two Southern Districts, also East and West. The greater the population density, the more federal courts a state will have. NY and California have four districts each, Vermont only has one. Judges are appointed by the US president, who has never spent time with any of them and appoints on the basis of anecdote and party affiliation.

Since Federal judges are appointed to serve in the district in which they established their careers, this means they bring all the defects, corrupt loyalties and politicized relationships to their new jurisdiction. Someone who was allowed to advance by virtue of a patronage at the County level will extend that loyalty to the Federal level, at the expense of the legal system.

Judge Donald Nugent made his career in the Cuyahoga County Prosecutor's office. Not only was he White Irish Catholic, but he was very publicized for his successful prosecution of a lunatic against whom even Marsha Clark and the O.J. team could have prevailed.

Don Nugent's star arrived as an undersized, brain damaged, cross-dressing loser named Frank Spisak. Frank fantasized he was a Nazi and aspired to kill black men in the name of Hitler. During his trial, Spisak sat on the stand wearing a Hitler mustache and chatted comfortably about his killings which he believed were "acts of God".

Spisak was damaged enough to have murdered a well-liked maintenance supervisor at Cleveland State University during daylight business hours in a campus washroom. The supervisor, Mr. Sheehan, an Irish national, had emigrated to America from the U.K. in pursuit of his future wife, Irish ex-pat, Kathleen. He happened to be in the vicinity while Spisak was shooting African-American minister Horace Rickerson, through a hole in a rest-room stall. Spisak felt potential witnesses needed to be mopped up and liquidated Sheehan, who left behind small children. Nice ones.

Spisak would have gotten away with the crime. He actually got away unseen then returned to the vicinity of the washroom where a crowd had assembled. He managed to self-destruct when a couple months later he got drunk and started shooting his gun from a window in his house. The police were called but still had no idea Spisak killed Rev. Rickerson. He was allowed to post bail and went home.

Some people just can't stand success. Spisak had been bragging about his murders and an anonymous party called the police. Ballistic tests proved that the gun used to kill Rev. Rickerson was the one Frank had been shooting out his window. Instead of hiding the evidence, Spisak made it publicly available.

The accumulation of Spisak's defects also included a head injury suffered during an auto accident. Assistant Prosecutor Nugent had the opportunity to posture as the Irish Vindicator against a party who basically convicted himself. The trial should have lasted five minutes, but Due Process gave Nugent the chance to publicize himself as an intolerant and uncompromising moralist. It was a stance for which he had to take no risks.

When presented with a real risk, Nugent wilted. When faced with an opportunity to protect a legal system, Nugent threw a paper tantrum and made sure the people who relied on him to vindicate rights, had no voice.

My federal filing asked the N. District of Ohio to recognize my right to appeal the order by which I was declared "vexatious" and banned from all state courts. The bases of this right were very direct.

First and most important, the judge who declared me "vexatious" and banned me from all Ohio courts forever didn't follow the procedure in the Ohio Vexatious Litigator statute. The statute requires a new filing with a new Complaint, Summons and Service. It can't be done by motion, which is what happened. Anything J. Lillian Greene ordered under those circumstances was void from the start and without jurisdiction. An order made without jurisdiction has no effect. A court can't even act without jurisdiction.

Second, the Ohio Constitution (Article I, section 16) gives access to all courts to all citizens of the state, Third, state Appellate Rules of Procedure 3 and 4 mandate an appeal if filed within 30 days. The 8th district accepted my appeal. The judges of the Cuyahoga County 8th District Court of Appeals accepted my filing fee, accepted my brief, set a briefing schedule for all parties and told me to drive in for oral arguments.

I was sure J. Nugent would be outraged on my behalf when he discovered a state court, under his nose, refused to hear a case it was obligated to conduct . . . especially one characterized by a vulgar and spectacular failure of intellect and intent by the office of J. Lillian Greene.

He wasn't. Nugent immediately banned me from the N. District Court of Ohio.

He did it on his own initiative and in violation of the most fundamental notions of Due Process and statutory procedure.

The "All Writs Act" is a long standing Congressional act which allows a Federal court to impose filing restrictions on a party who is "abusing" the legal process. The definition of "abuse" has never been clearly ascertained, even though it should have been. For example, it could be very easy to impose filing restrictions against a particular party who has re-filed a case that was already dismissed (*res judicata*, collateral *estoppel*, Civil Rule 12). Or to prevent a party from re-filing the same motion or relitigating an issue that was already decided in a case.

If you give a person with an advantage the opportunity to enlarge themselves at the expense of someone else, they tend to do so. If you give a judge the power to completely misappropriate someone's legal power, there are people exhilarated by doing so.

The problem with Nugent's application of filing restrictions under the All Writs Act was serious. The act requires notice and hearing prior to the imposition of restrictions. If you read the 9th circuit federal case "DeLong v. Hennessey", one can see the hearing requirement. This rule has been followed in other federal jurisdictions.

"The Ninth Circuit reviews vexatious litigant orders under a four-part test established in "DeLong v. Hennessey", 912 F.2d The test requires that the trial court afford the plaintiff minimum due process notice, an opportunity to be heard, and an adequate record for review, which should include a showing "that the litigant's activities were numerous and abusive." and the order must be "narrowly tailored to closely fit the specific vice encountered." (DeLong at 1147–48.)

It's called Due Process and is described in the 5th and 14th Amendments. In addition, filing restrictions under the Act are limited to illegal behaviors against a particular party related to one particular set of facts or transaction. A court can't impose filing restrictions against a party concerning all future suits. (See "Cromer v Kraft Foods" 225 F.3d 653).

Nugent didn't care. Nugent issued an order saying I was never allowed to file in the N. District of Ohio unless I made a motion to his court, with copies of the Complaint from every suit I had ever filed to date in any court in the United States, with the accompanying order and final disposition for all those suits. That is hundreds of documents.

This was a criminal violation by a brutal narcissist who knew no one would hold him accountable. I made a Motion to Reconsider and pointed out the language in the statute and the Due Process violations which made his order void. Nugent didn't care. He disregarded the language of the All Writs Act which required "notice and hearing" prior to filing restrictions, "Cromer v Kraft Foods", ibid and authority which states that any order which violates Constitutional procedure is void and entered without jurisdiction.

Nugent had to protect the people who made him. These were the institutions of Cuyahoga County and the regional Irish Catholic political organizations. When called upon to do something integral, Nugent just resorted to unfair advantage and the principle of partisan loyalty. Protect your friends. Kill your enemy.

Fixing this would be truly easy. The Federal Appellate Court will see right through this. There can't be failure all the way up to the threshold of the US Supreme Court. Right? An appeal in the 6th circuit involved a jurisdiction with four states. Surely they could read the provision of the All Writs Act and case law construing it.

I made an appeal to the 6th circuit and filed a complaint with the Judicial Misconduct Board. It's easier to skate on a buffalo chip than get a judge disciplined. The misconduct complaint was received by Judge Alice Batchelder who was from Medina, Ohio, a town just outside Cleveland. Her husband, William, is the Speaker for the Ohio House of representatives and is also from Medina. The misconduct complaint was disregarded.

The 6th circuit dismissed my appeal under the "Rooker-Feldman" doctrine. "Rooker-Feldman" is a doctrine which says a party can't re-litigate a case he/she has already lost in state court, in federal court. There was no prior state filing. The original filing for purposes of appeal was in Federal Court. There had to have been a state proceeding which examined and wrote an order responsive to the issues sought to be litigated again in federal court, for "Rooker" to apply. However, the original filing was in Federal Court.

This was truly the product of political inbreeding which produced an epidemic of Down's Syndrome. I was dealing with minds steeped in nitric acid. I couldn't avoid the casual and regular expressions of a failed and corrupt judiciary. The "All Writs Act" only has application in federal court. There had been no state proceeding. The original filing was in Federal Court. It was impossible to raise my issues in state court because a state court has no jurisdiction to hear or use the "All Writs Act". Even a bad judge wouldn't draft a court order like this. The court couldn't tell a cat from a car.

I called an attorney and asked how this could be possible. Had the 6th circuit extended its affirmative action programs to include those who endured severe head injury?

The order induced motion sickness in my attorney pal:

"Wow. That's breathtaking. Really bad. Sounds like the judge told his staff attorney to get rid of the case. He probably told him/her to just say anything because the US Supreme Court will never grant review anyway. (The US Supreme Court only accepts between 2% and 5% of applications for review) You keep missing the point. Judges give rulings to well established attorneys they know. Judges don't like *pro se* litigants. They hold them in contempt. They're supposed to be nicer to them, but are really meaner. Plus, you're an outsider they don't know. They've never seen you before and won't again. You're just an inconvenience they can afford to shortchange. And, you are asking them to find serious fault with another judge. The irony is the worse the mistake, the more it gets excused because judges don't want to maintain a standard that could be used against them some day."

"Yeah, but how could the other two members of the panel sign that filth?" (federal circuit cases can be heard by a panel of three. A lead judge will do most of the work and write the opinion, which is normally approved on a pro forma basis by the other two judges.)

"They don't care. They don't even read the order or the briefs. They just follow the lead justice to make sure the lead will sign their orders if they are assigned together on a panel again. You're not part of a group they recognize. It's not fair but you have to stop expecting quality from government employees. Judges are willing to do an enormous amount of damage. It's trite, but fools have themselves as attorneys. It's not because people who represent themselves are necessarily incompetent. If judges bothered to read your stuff, they would see you are at least their peer. It's because judges give preferential status to attorneys acting on behalf of a client and much more preference to attorneys they know. They also will find any excuse to get rid of cases. They are overworked.

It's a tiered system. Judges discriminate on the basis of status. It's completely illegal and someone should remind judges Clay and Cole about this. As African-Americans, they should know what happens when you discriminate on the basis of status rather than quality.

Anyway, you've given real pearls to real swine. Virtue has no forum. Self-interest does. When will you stop? It's killing you."

I wasn't just paranoid. Well, maybe I was. A paranoid is a person with all the facts. Maybe paranoia is a virtue and a necessary adaptation.

See the quote below from a researched article:

> "Appellate judges have adjusted their practices and even their rules to resolve more cases and to do so more quickly, often at the expense of merits consideration. For example, circuits have increased their reliance on staff attorneys to screen cases and suggest decisions, have limited the time for oral argument and even its availability, and have strictly enforced

technical rules to move cases off the docket."; citing, Hon. Richard J. Cardamone, Foreword: How an Expanding Caseload Impacts Federal Appellate Procedures, 65 BROOK. L. REV. 281 (1999);

Even more. The 6th circuit loses all the time before the US Supreme Court. See excerpts from the December 2012 "ABA journal":

"The 6th Circuit, based in Cincinnati, has had a particularly dismal record before the high court. In the seven Supreme Court terms completed since the fall of 2005, the 6th Circuit has been reversed 31 out of 38 times, for an 81.6 percent reversal rate, based on figures compiled by two Philadelphia lawyers. That leads all the federal circuits for that time period, with the 9th Circuit coming in as the second most reversed—100 out of 128 cases, or 78.1 percent . . ."

"In February 2011, the Cincinnati Enquirer said the 6th Circuit was "suffering through a major slump" and "keeps getting the law wrong." Those observations appeared before the 6th Circuit was reversed five more times in the spring of 2011, not to mention the five (out of five) of its decisions reversed in the Supreme Court's 2011-12 term . . ."

In one case, the high court reversed the 6th Circuit's decision that a teacher at a religious school was covered by the "ministerial exception" to the civil rights laws. The 6th Circuit "committed three errors" in its legal analysis, Chief Justice John G. Roberts Jr. said in the unanimous Jan. 11 opinion."

I spoke with a federal judge in Michigan about this. His response was to cite his special contempt for Ohio judges.

I filed a Writ of *Certiorari* in the US Supreme Court. This is an expensive and peculiar endeavor. The US Supreme Court insists that Writ applications be in pamphlet form. All orders and the contents of the Appendix have to be re-typed in a format specified by the Court Rules. An applicant needs 40 copies. The pamphlet has to be made by a professional printer. You can't do it at home. The procedure is time consuming and expensive.

Review was denied. The courts not only failed to protect an 87 year old widow, but managed to fine and punish the party who sought to protect her. It also made sure he had no voice in state or federal courts.

A national failure of coordinated intent.

20

Danger Bar and Deferred Action
Steal That Evidence

"The corrupt always refer to morality and rules. They're great devices."

An accumulation of people were staring at me. Why was the attorney for my mother's trustee in the room? Had someone finally decided to expose his deceit and theft against my mother? I must have lost consciousness for a moment because a roomful of attorneys associated with a Washington State Bar disciplinary action, were waiting for me to say something. I asked Bar prosecutor, Linda Eide, to repeat her question or restate whatever could have happened in the interlude during which I had a stress related absence.

Almost four years after my initial conversation with Washington State Bar Association representative, Doug Ende, the Washington State Bar Office of Disciplinary Counsel (ODC), decided to act on the anonymous letter from Cleveland and bring a Formal Complaint against me. Don't they have a statute of limitations? I proved I was being chased by a corrupt Cleveland administration for exposing corruption. Why didn't Bar give me a prize? Why didn't they name an office room in my honor after being prosecuted for exercising my 1st Amendment rights and publicizing a failed Ohio administration?

I didn't expect to be here. In summer of 2010 I called the Washington Bar to complain about the attorney who was helping my mother's Trustee commit theft against my geriatric mother. He had refused to comply with court orders to distribute property and had taken unauthorized attorney fees from her trust. In response, the Bar brought charges against me and used Trustee's attorney as a witness. The anonymous letter from Cleveland had been sitting on someone's desk for a long time.

I had to attend this procedure by myself. I couldn't get an attorney. There are attorneys who specialize in defense against ethical charges and I spoke with several of them, including Anne Seidell, Leland Ripley, Steve Smith and a couple others. They all worked for the Office of Disciplinary Counsel in the past. They all refused representation.

Steve Smith was an attorney from Idaho and had been Chief Disciplinary Counsel for the ODC (office of disciplinary counsel) in Washington state. It's common in that region for attorneys to work between Washington, Oregon and Idaho. Steve asked me to send my pleadings and defenses. He also asked me to send a retainer. While I was accumulating the money, Steve called to say:

"I can't take this case. There are only a handful of people in the world who understand how this really works in Washington State, and you aren't one of them. You are going to get hammered at the hearing and there is nothing you can do about it. It doesn't matter how good your case is and how bad Bar's is, you are going to lose. It would be cheating to take your money."

I tried to enjoin the hearing. The Federal District court abstained, which means it didn't find for or against me, but deferred to the scheduled state proceeding. I filed for a Writ of Prohibition in state court. Prohibition is meant to stop an action conducted without jurisdiction. I claimed the ODC had no jurisdiction since I had done nothing in Washington state as an attorney. There was no territorial or long arm jurisdiction. The state court judge said the Bar had complete immunity since it was part of the Washington Supreme Court. This was a contemptible failure by the state court. Judges are subject to injunction when they have no jurisdiction or to stop an unconstitutional procedure. It's the famous law of "Ex Parte Young", *supra*. The state court judge wasn't familiar with the case.

I tried again at the Washington Supreme Court which also has original jurisdiction for writs. The case was decided, without hearing, by the Clerk of Courts. The clerk is not a judge under the Washington Constitution. Why don't they just give cases they don't like to the janitor?

Bar's Formal Complaint asked for "Probation". During a settlement conversation, Bar prosecutor, Linda Eide offered three years of suspension. Why suspension if the Complaint asked for "Probation"? In addition, I had done nothing with my license in Washington. I had been inactive and had not represented clients in Washington state. Bar had no jurisdiction or venue over me. Inactive attorneys are only liable for unauthorized practice of law within the state of their bar.

I cooperated with the pre-hearing investigation and proved that I had done nothing wrong in Ohio and that I wasn't there at the time of an alleged crime. Bar had my ATM receipts showing I was in Vermont and New Hampshire during the time in question. It also had a copy of the "No Bill" returned by the Ohio Grand Jury, which proved I didn't do anything.

I showed Bar that everyone connected with my Ohio case, (with the exception of Cuyahoga County Clerk of Criminal Courts Mark Lime, who was indicted after my hearing), had been arrested, convicted and sent to jail.

Linda Eide didn't care. She refused to acknowledge evidence. My filings in state and federal court offended her sense of control. I had to fly to Seattle for the hearing. Bar was holding my license hostage. The Hearing Officer refused to rule on my jurisdictional motions or any other motion for the prior four months.

The proceeding was held in the offices of ODC. It was a conventional downtown office space with large rooms to accommodate its hearings. The American Bar Association had been insisting that Disciplinary proceedings should not be conducted by Bar employees, but Washington state disregarded the advice.

It was good advice and based on a fundamental principle of America law known as Separation of Powers. Separation of Powers acknowledges that concentrations of power in one entity will corrupt an organization and allow it to exercise unfair advantage. American separation of powers insists that one group cannot combine executive (appointment), judicial and legislative (rule making) power, which is exactly what the design of Bar disciplinary proceedings do.

Bar has adopted a design for its proceedings more similar to governments in Cuba, Nazi Germany and Stalinist Russia. Bar chooses the people who screen ethical complaints from third parties. This is like choosing the members of a Grand Jury. It then proceeds to appoint its own prosecutor from its own employees. This prosecutor is responsible for the conduct of the case and all decisions prior to the appointment of a Hearing Officer. The Hearing Officer is chosen by Bar from a list of people it knows, who are all bar members and in many cases, affiliated with other Bar committees and activities. Bar also writes its own rules of conduct and procedure in conjunction with the state Supreme Court. The Supreme Court sends its representative, the Clerk of Courts, to sit in on rule making deliberations. So, Bar appoints its own Grand Jury, Prosecutor, Judge and writes its own rules.

After a Hearing Officer makes a determination, a review is available. This review committee is a body of 12 people unilaterally chosen by the Bar. It is run by a Chair who not only rules on motions during this review process, but who also votes in the final determination of the Review Committee. The judge is part of the jury.

If litigants don't like the results of the Review Committee vote, they can appeal to the Washington Supreme Court, which is the "boss" of Disciplinary Counsel and has complete administrative responsibility for the conduct and procedures of Disciplinary actions. The process which has been controlled by the Supreme Court and run by its employees, comes back to the Supreme Court.

In short, Bar illegally controls every aspect of Disciplinary actions. It also reviews itself and controls the administrative and clerical staff responsible for creating a record. It can hide or distort anything it wants. ODC counsel start at around $100,000.00 per year. They are bought to cheat.

I called a senior attorney in the area who went to Yale law. He was very friendly and described the prevailing hatred against ODC. In every other state in which I worked, disciplinary counsel was not even a topic of conversation. In Washington State, it was a prominent part of every small practice attorney's consciousness.

The attorney explained the history of ODC. He said during the 1980s, ethical practice in Washington state had deteriorated badly and there was an accumulation of ethical complaints that needed to be addressed. At the time, ODC was very small and didn't have a staff to accommodate the quantity of violations that had accumulated. During the '90s, a decision was made to increase the staff to manage disciplinary complaints and the backlog of cases was eliminated.

In the meantime, the attorneys who were hired to dispose of the accumulation had no where to go. They weren't good attorneys or good minds and had no lateral mobility. No one in private practice wanted them. So, instead of liquidating the office or reducing its scale, the Supreme Court allowed ODC to remain as a large interest group which needed to find defects in order to maintain its salaries. A staff of over 20 people became a self-perpetuating entity whose jobs were primarily keeping their jobs.

Since ODC was only accountable to itself, it started violating every legal principle on which American jurisprudence is based. It targeted solo practitioners and extorted "legal charges" for investigations from attorneys who had been targeted. Several attorneys tell stories of being targeted by the bar for offenses based on rules that have no objective meaning ("Frivolous Conduct") and being forced to pay thousands of dollars for bar "investigation and legal fees" to accept a public "Reprimand", in lieu of a hearing and possible disbarment or suspension.

The hatred against Office of Disciplinary Counsel became an established part of Washington legal culture. But, like the Gestapo, it was desperately feared and no one would challenge it. It represented the corporatism of the Washington legal system which had displaced jurisprudence. The legal system of Washington state had devolved into an accumulation of groups which had greater or lesser access to income by way of the police power. It no longer had a view of life or a social philosophy; it became a means to distribute income among favored people.

Typical ODC behavior included sanctioning a party for writing a satirical poem about the Washington Supreme Court (the case of Anton Miller), chasing a party for 2 years without good cause and hiding exculpatory evidence favorable to the accused (Karen Unger) and refusing to bring an action against larger firms. Almost all ODC actions targeted solo and small practitioners.

It was also notorious for second guessing courts. An action which was not sanctioned or punished in court, could become the basis for a Bar disciplinary action if it didn't like a motion someone made. Bar became the pre-filing censor for legal dialogue. This violated the 1st Amendment and a party's right of court access. It's an outrageous and authoritarian usurpation of the intellectual exchange and dialogue which has to go on in courts to examine ideas. Someone always loses a motion. It's a party's right to be wrong. Judges make mistakes. That is why we have two levels of appeal and supervising federal courts.

What started as a temporary means to liquidate an accumulation of cases became an institutionalized expression and enforcement of a failed legal culture. Corporatism and group maintenance replaced American Constitutional notions of justice. The dreary white people of Washington state managed to remove ethics from their legal system by enlarging an entity charged with enforcing Constitutional ethics. Like most evil, it was banal and done in camera.

Prior to hearing, I wrote a bar representative named Ted Stiles. Ted was an ODC affiliate charged with reviewing Hearing Officer decisions on a pre-hearing basis. His persona kept changing. At times he was E.E. Stiles. He could also be T. Stiles the II. I guess he felt the power and biological thrust of his dynastic presence. A photo of him looked like Fido Dido, a person who saw without comprehending.

I became acquainted with him during the motion practice prior to hearing. I moved him to review the Hearing Officer's refusal to rule on my jurisdictional motions to dismiss. Ted ruled that she didn't have to and that I had nothing to fear at hearing. "There would be ample opportunity to explain everything in your case."

I exhausted my alternatives and had to attend hearing. I flew to Seattle and stayed in a motel run by an Indian family. I took the commuter train to the downtown offices and met my prosecutor, Linda Eide, for the first time. She was a plain and rodent faced woman with a layered accumulation of fat. Linda was the kind of person who adapted her life as a subordinate to power. She was the type who would volunteer to organize footnotes and annotations for a Law Review project, while everyone else competed to participate in the substantive legal analysis. The hearing officer was an unlikely blonde simian with undersized nostrils, narrow eyes and a mouth that pushed forward aggressively. I didn't expect much from her. The cuffs of her over-length sleeves touched her palms as she typed busily. Her notions of couture were rural.

I moved to dismiss the case because there was no jurisdiction. This was the issue I had been raising for the past nine months. She said "no".

I asked her to remove herself on the basis of bias. She looked at me as if I couldn't have said what I just said. She stared angrily at me prior to a reply. Her breathing apparatus flexed and she said "no".

Preliminaries had barely ended when Bar amended its Complaint at hearing without notice, motion or court permission. It added eight charges unmentioned in its Complaint and changed its desired sanction from "Probation" to "Disbarment".

The Complaint is not a moving target. It can't be amended at hearing. See "In re Ruffalo", 390 US 544, which states that a party is stuck with the contents of his Complaint which can't be changed during trial.

As it turned out, ODC didn't care about rules or evidence. It didn't care about civil procedure, perjury, obstruction of justice, Due Process, the 6th Amendment or really anything at all except creating a record against me.

The Trustee's attorney was called to the stand. How could the person who facilatated deceit at the expense of a 93 year old widow suffering from Alzheimer's, be awarded an advantage and immunity from an organization sworn to protect legal ethics? How could anyone favor him over the son protecting his mother?

Linda Eide questioned him about an alleged offense which wasn't in the Complaint. The charge involved a subpoena I issued on behalf of my mother for back accountings required by law. My mother's trustee had neglected annual accountings to hide the massive amounts of money he had been removing from her Trust.

ODC claimed I had no right to issue a subpoena and used fraud to get the court to provide it. I was completely surprised by the charge. Due Process insists that a party know of all charges before hearing so he can organize a defense. It's a simple Constitutional notion of fairness codified into our laws. Not only that, but any party to a case can issue a subpoena. I was *pro se* in a case and issued a subpoena subsequent to Civil Rule 45, which says, any party to a lawsuit can issue a subpoena. An attorney *pro se* has all the rights of a licensed attorney.

Trustee's attorney calmly cooperated with Linda Eide and created the impression that because I signed my subpoena motion with my state bar number, I was fraudulently representing myself as an attorney to get a subpoena. Eide kept claiming that only licensed and active attorneys can issue subpoenas. Since I was inactive, I couldn't issue a subpoena and had to misrepresent my credential to get one. It was a shameless contrivance. I objected to the misstatement of the law and to a surprise Complaint amendment at trial. The Hearing Officer disregarded my objection.

The subpoena was issued years ago. A judge and 2 commissioners knew of it. It was issued without objection by Trustee's attorney or any of the judges and commissioners.

ODC amended its Complaint eight times during the course of the hearing. It also found offense with some motions I filed in Vermont. Motion practice in other states was none of its business. A party has the right to file without worrying about what someone else thinks. It's part of free speech and the healthy and privileged intellectual exchange that goes on in court. There were no sanctions or penalties associated with the Vermont motions. A Washington state administrative hearing has no jurisdiction or venue for events in Vermont.

I had the right of access to Courts under the 1st Amendment. Is Washington state bar the new censor which decides what can be said in court and what can't? These contrivances were taking on the character of a dirty Witch Hunt.

I calmly laid out my case and entered 42 exhibits proving I wasn't in Ohio at the time alleged in the Ohio charges against me four years earlier in 2007, that other charges on which Bar relied were dismissed with a finding of "Not Guilty" on my behalf and that everyone involved in the Ohio cases were removed from office and/ or in jail.

The evidence also included letters of defense and commendation from attorneys, the former Vermont Deputy Secretary of State and a very distinguished person who clerked for Supreme Court Justice Souter.

This same evidence and exhibits were provided to the Bar prior to hearing and over 80 pages of transcript, during the hearing. They were identified, re-numbered by the Hearing Officer to accommodate her numbering sequence and given to the Bar clerk, Allison Sato, who promised she would not get them confused or lose them.

Between testimony and case presentations, we all had access to the embellished provisions of the bar. The catering was in stark contrast to the legal quality of the proceedings. These included expensive coffees, designer chocolates, dishes of premium nuts, bottled beverages, tea and fruit. They were free and available all the time. A woman from the white service class of Seattle kept the kitchen tidy. The mentality of the food service was confusing. It was generous and to human measure. It gave one the impression that this was a meeting to work things out comfortably. After which, we could all return to the consensus and common activities in which we all participated before. "No need to worry. We'll figure this out. No one will get hurt needlessly. Chocolate?"

Bar counsel Linda Eide, closed her case by asking the Hearing Officer to disregard the filed Complaint and to disbar me. I objected and said all penalties were limited to those articulated on the Complaint, which were limited to "Probation". Since I had done nothing wrong and proved I wasn't in Ohio at the time of the alleged offense, No Penalty, was the proper finding.

After a day and a half, the hearing closed and I went home.

Stolen Record

Three weeks later, I got a copy of the hearing record. All my exhibits and documentary proof had been removed from the record. All 42 exhibits were gone. All of Bar's exhibits were listed on the record. All of mine were gone. All my evidence had been removed. Documentary and physical evidence is much stronger than testimony. It goes to Burden of Proof and Production. This was a filthy and criminal tactic. You can't remove contents of a record. It's like removing drugs from the evidence room in a police station.

ODC has two affiliations. It is part of the Washington state bar and at the same time, administered by the state Supreme Court. Bar is in the habit of claiming judicial immunity even when it is not acting as a judge. It has been allowed to say no one could hold them accountable since they were part of the Washington Supreme Court. This is completely wrong. Judicial immunity only applies for activities during trial. It doesn't give someone the right to steal evidence. The Bar didn't have immunity, but I couldn't get a judge in Washington state to recognize their accountability. No one would apply law against the bar.

I called the State Attorney General. He said, "I'm not surprised by anything you tell me about ODC, but we don't prosecute, we defend state entities."

I called to confront ODC. An attorney from the bar explained that they were never entered into evidence and had no legal existence. I asked him about the 80 pages of transcript over which all the exhibits were entered. I asked him about state rule RPC 3.3 and 3.4 which says Bar has to acknowledge all exculpatory evidence of which it knows, whenever and however it is provided. I also asked him about "Brady v Maryland" 373 US 83, which states that a prosecutor has to acknowledge all exculpatory evidence known to it at any time, before, during and after hearing. I also asked him about the Washington state statutes on perjury, obstruction of justice and case law on spoliation of evidence.

Spoliation has been defined as the willful destruction of evidence or the failure to preserve potential evidence for another's use in pending or future litigation. "Trigon Ins. Co. v. U.S.", 204 F.R.D.277, (E.D.Va., 2001). Washington spoliation law has its expression in "Pier 67, Inc. v. King County", 89 Wn.2d 379;

> "There", said the court, "our Supreme Court reaffirmed the evidentiary conclusion that when a party fails to produce relevant evidence without satisfactory explanation, the only inference which the finder of fact may draw is that such evidence would be unfavorable to him." 133 Wn. App. at 898.

Bar Counsel informed me their rules did not include "Brady" or "Ruffalo" rights. He didn't know about "Pier 67" or the Washington state obstruction of justice statutes. Bar ODC is not an affiliate of the American Constitution.

These rights aren't optional. They are imposed by US Supreme Court cases which apply standards to every state. Participation in the Constitution is not discretionary. All parties have "constructive" or presumed knowledge of Constitutional law and state statutes. Federal statutes of obstructing justice and conspiracy to violate civil rights would apply too.

There is also the fact that Bar proceedings are administrative in nature and are controlled by the state Administrative Procedures Act. The standard for admissible evidence is low, very low. It's harder to keep evidence out of an administrative hearing than to get it in. An administrative hearing will allow anything, including hearsay, that is relevant. See RCW 34.05.452. It's a much lower standard of evidence than the one for trials in state courts.

I called a Harvard grad in California, who had defended clients in Washington state bar proceedings. He hated the bar and said everybody did. Since he was prone to monologue, I just listened to him:

"Do you know the case of Karen Unger? Washington ODC chased her for two years until someone finally threw her case out. It cost her tens of thousands. Bar hid evidence in her case too. How about Anton Miller? Miller wrote a satirical poem about the Washington Supreme Court and the ODC disciplined him. There's no 1st Amendment in Washington state.

They always do this. Their rules are vague and would never stand a Constitutional examination, but everyone is so frightened of them, no one will challenge the Bar. If you challenge the Bar, they'll come after you. They only attack sole practitioners and threaten accumulating money charges for the cost of their "investigations" until you accept whatever they want. When someone tries to sue them, which is very rare, they claim they have judicial immunity because they are administered by the State Supreme Court.

Of course, this is bullshit because even judges are subject to injunctions and Constitutional claims for unconstitutional acts, but the state is so politicized, that the state judges won't allow cases to be heard against them. The State judges will flat out say they have no jurisdiction. It's a fucking lie, but an institutionalized one. Washington is a third world country when it comes to the law. It's also bad that no one recognizes the difference between when a judge acts in an administrative capacity and when he/she acts to adjudicate disputes. There is no immunity from when a court acts as an administrator. It's so stupid I could scream, but in Washington state they would make up a crime against screaming.

Look into "Separation of Powers". Bar is a seminar in how to violate it. An organization can't be its own prosecutor, judge, rule writer and selector of the parties who perform these functions. Bar is even its own Grand Jury. The Washington Bar chooses the panel of people who decide if a case should have a formal complaint.

Washington state has become Brazil. If your attorney is connected, you can steal from your mother, ask damages for the amount of time it took to steal and get them from a judge without even going to court.

You know what's even worse, the Washington Supreme Court protects the Bar. The Bar prosecutor in the "Unger" case wasn't fired. She was retained for several more years. This happens all the time. The Supreme Court never revises rules or notices that they are comically illegal.

Real information is secret and inside. Someone in the Supreme Court WANTS the Bar to behave this way. I have to think that the Supreme Court wants to posture on ethics at the expense of small people who are defenseless.

You can't win against them. They have no rules or limitations. ODC is an interest group whose primary job is to keep their jobs by inventing fault and conducting investigations and hearings for which respondents are charged.

Someone needs to blow them up, but everyone is too terrified to say anything

I gotta go, big client arrived, but before I do, check the background of your Hearing Officer. I'll bet anything she has some special relationship with the bar."

My Hearing Officer was Lisa Hammel. Nothing about her came up on Google, but I discovered she worked at a firm called Williams and Williams. I looked them up. Turns out her boss, Kinnon Williams, was on the Bar Judicial Selection Committee. This alone was grounds to find a conflict of interest. Hammel should have removed herself from the case. Bar never should have chosen her. I looked further. She had acted as a hearing officer for Bar before. Office of Disciplinary Counsel knew what they'd get from her.

I knew nothing about the organization of ODC and its relation to the Washington state Bar. It was time to become educated. I still had to endure an appeal of whatever the Hearing Officer found after all my evidence had been removed from the record.

ODC is an office within the Washington State Bar Association. Although it is named as part of the Washington state bar, it is administered by the Washington Supreme Court and is directly accountable to it. It has a permanent staff of attorneys who have made careers conducting attorney discipline against primarily sole practitioners. In conjunction with the Washington Supreme Court, ODC drafts its own substantive and procedural rules for attorney discipline, appoints its own prosecutors and hearing officers to conduct disciplinary hearings, chooses the panel of state bar members to do appellate review of hearing officer decisions and then conducts the last stage of review in the Supreme Court, of which ODC is the agent.

Separation of Powers insists that a state actor cannot combine executive, judicial and legislative powers, which is exactly what ODC does when it writes its own rules, appoints its own prosecutors and judges to hear disciplinary actions and acts as its own judicial body during the initial hearing and the first review. All participants in Bar disciplinary proceedings are state bar members.

Because of its affiliation with the Washington Supreme Court, ODC will claim it is exempt from external Constitutional scrutiny due to judicial immunity. There is no blanket immunity. My Harvard pal was right. One only has to consult "Ex Parte Young" 209 US 123, "Hafer v Melo", and 42 US 1983, among many other authorities which are designed to impose the principle that a party can't use state or judicial affiliation to commit crimes, torts and to violate the Constitution.

It is also important to distinguish between the Washington Supreme Court when it acts in its judicial capacity and when it acts in its administrative capacity. When the Supreme Court acts as an administrator and allows Disciplinary Counsel to use unconstitutional rules, hide evidence and retain corrupt employees, it has no immunity.

Washington Procedure vs. California

One can contrast the Washington disciplinary procedure with that of California to see confirmation of Washington Constitutional defects. California conducts attorney discipline in independent courts which are not affiliated with the Bar. The rules are drafted by the California legislature and judges are appointed by parties independent of the California State Bar Association. The appointing parties include the governor, the Speaker of the Assembly and The Senate Committee on Rules. Review is also done in courts independent of the California state bar.

American Bar Association Wants Attorney Discipline Removed from Bar

The American Bar Association has been recommending that attorney discipline be removed from state bar associations for years. It reviewed the Washington state discipline procedure in 2006 and advised that it should remove attorney discipline from the Bar and appoint an oversight committee. It also told the Washington state Bar to fund discipline hearings from Bar Dues and not charges against Respondents. The Washington bar met 2 years later to examine these recommendations and rejected both of them "because the system is working so well as it stands".

Pg. 18 of Report "**. . . the team recommends cessation of the Association's role in funding the disciplinary system from its budget. The Court should fund the disciplinary agency via a direct annual assessment on lawyers for the discipline system . . .**" Pg. 19 of Report

This is consistent with ABA recommendations for all state Bars. See the short excerpt below from an American Bar Association review of the New Hampshire state attorney disciplinary procedure. It "strongly" advises that members of the

Attorney Discipline Office not be employees of the New Hampshire state bar. Note that the New Hampshire Attorney Discipline Office (ADO) is neither an employee of the New Hampshire Bar Association nor the judicial branch. In Washington State, ODC is both an employee of the Washington State Bar Association and simultaneously an agent/employee of the Washington Supreme Court:

"OUTLINE OF ABA REPORT ON NEW HAMPSHIRE LAWYER DISCIPLINARY SYSTEM

The ABA . . . "strongly encourages that ADO personnel not be considered employees of NH Bar Association."

End of Excerpt

Findings from the People's Democratic Republic of Bar

It was much worse than I could have imagined. The Hearing Officer, Lisa Hammel, made up offenses and falsified the record in her "Findings of Fact and Recommendations". She was unconcerned that Linda Eide removed all my evidence from the files.

Hammel claimed that I committed a felony under Lakewood Ohio Municipal Code 549.04(c). Were we both at the same hearing?

Ohio Revised Code 549.04 is a misdemeanor statute. 549.04(c) is a misdemeanor of the 4th degree which is the lowest misdemeanor in Ohio. It involves improper storage of a firearm and doesn't concern Bar discipline. Lakewood Ohio Municipal Court only has misdemeanor jurisdiction. It can't hear felony charges.

In response to my 6th Amendment defenses that I couldn't compel witnesses to attend from foreign states because the Washington state subpoena power didn't extend beyond Washington state, Hammel said;

"It doesn't matter because Bar can't subpoena these witnesses either."

Hammel disregarded my jurisdiction and venue arguments.

Hammel made no reference to the evidence Bar removed from the record.

Hammel made no reference to the fact that I had never been subject to discipline and cooperated completely with ODC.

She made no reference to the delay between alleged events and the Hearing.

She made no reference to the four letters of recommendation which were in the record.

Things like delay, letters of recommendation, absence of prior discipline, cooperation during investigation, etc. are codified in the Washington state Bar Rules as "Mitigators". Mitigators significantly reduce the penalty to which a Respondent can be subject.

I trusted the Bar and fell into its institutionalized trap.

First Review

ODC assigned a different attorney for its review. He was a sexless person named Craig Bray. Bray had a sagging chin and permanently moist lips that were unevenly pursed. He gave the impression of unsavory moisture and involuntary accumulations of saliva into his collar. In a just world, he would have been arrested for impersonating a man. The hearing was held in March of 2012.

ODC is consistent in its failures. A party is not disbarred by the Hearing Officer. Only the State Supreme Court can remove a license. Subsequent to presentment before the Supreme Court, ODC has a first level of review, conducted in its own offices, by people ODC chooses to hear appeals. The composition of the Review Board is eight attorneys and four lay people.

The attorneys are all Bar members with whom ODC has a working relation. They can be former hearing officers and are parties who have participated in disciplinary proceedings. (I researched the roster. At least two of my board members had been Hearing Officers) A Chair is appointed by the Bar. The Chair organizes the Review Board and has the right to vote on a sanction. My Chair was a man named Thomas Waite. Mr. Waite had also been responsible for ruling on motions during the appellate process. This means the Chair was acting as a judge and part of the jury. He ruled for Bar in every one of my motions.

The lay parties have no knowledge of law and are incompetent to have any legal opinions or determine the fate of anyone. They are completely subject to the consensus of attorneys. To have four lay people act where four attorneys could have been is to substitute one third of the voting members qualified to understand arguments in a Respondent's favor with those who are not qualified to have any legal opinion.

Mr. Waite had been a corporate attorney. He was pale and partisan in a deliberate and formed manner. Waite knew how to disappear as an individual and only act in reference to what his organization needed. There was always a rule which absolved him of responsibility to choose a view of life.

Appeals have special rules. One of them concerns the record. The facts are limited to the record of the trial hearing. If ODC managed to limit the record to its own evidence by hiding all of mine, the only thing a review board can consider is evidence in favor of Bar. Lying and deceit create real advantages. I had to go into the appeal with a stolen record and Hearing Officer Findings which seemed to be unrelated to testimony in the original hearing.

During my presentation to the board, I stated the jurisdictional and venue defects of the Bar's case. I showed I was not in Ohio at the time alleged and couldn't have been guilty of anything. I cited the 42 exhibits stolen from the record. I demonstrated the difference between the sanction of "Probation" on the original complaint and Bar's illegal request for disbarment at hearing. I mentioned the other eight surprise Complaint amendments.

Opposing counsel objected to say that my evidence was not in the record and I couldn't make reference to things that weren't there. Theft by the Bar didn't count. They disregarded the law that says hidden evidence is presumed to be in favor of an accused and has to be acknowledged before, during and after hearing. Everyone affiliated with Bar also disregarded the rule that EVERYTHING is evidence in an administrative hearing. It uses a very liberal standard of evidence. Even hearsay is allowable. The term "scintilla of relevance" is the standard. It's almost impossible to keep anything OUT of an administrative hearing.

When I demonstrated that I had done nothing in Washington state and that case law says bar status by itself is not sufficient for jurisdiction to attach, one of the board members became resentful. He didn't understand the limits of Territorial Jurisdiction and the idea that procedural due process also involves substantive notions of fairness. It's not fair to try someone in a place far away from where he could call witnesses or in a place where he had conducted no activity. I guess he didn't know about "federalism". The panel didn't stir when I cited the limitations of the Washington state Long Arm Statute which is decisive about what behaviors attach jurisdiction to a state. The same applies for the Washington state venue statute which only allows hearings in the county where an offense took place.

When I pointed out that Bar's own rules prohibited a hearing in Washington state if the Respondent was neither a resident nor found in the state, Bray said:

"Well, we would have had the hearing in Vermont. It just would have cost more".

The Bible is correct; the Last have become First.

Washington state courts and administrative hearings have no right to convene in Vermont. They have no jurisdiction outside of Washington State. This is fundamental and is a limitation for every state in the union. A New Hampshire court cannot try you for theft in Rhode Island.

With the exception of articulated resentment from Mr. Broome (a Hearing Officer for ODC in the past), the panel was silent. There were no sounds of exasperation or sympathy when I described the evidence Linda Eide stole. No one cared about my efforts to expose corruption in Ohio. No one's eyes rolled when I described how a surprise amendment to the Complaint from "Probation" to "Disbarment" (and the other eight surprise charges first revealed at hearing), violated Civil Rule 15, "In re Ruffalo", (supra), the 5th Amendment (notice of charges and penalties) and every notion of fair play which accompanies American legal theory.

Bray explained to the panel that "our rules allow us to amend the Complaint whenever we want". The autonomous region of "Baristan" had exempted itself from the Constitution.

Blank looks accompanied venue and jurisdiction defenses. They weren't addressed. The most fundamental things were disregarded.

Steve Smith was right. The attorney who turned down my case knew the Bar. My fate had been decided in summer of 2011, months before I attended the first September hearing.

The board affirmed the Hearing Officer recommendations. They weren't unanimous. A silent member acknowledged my jurisdiction, venue and delay arguments.

Second Review

Disciplinary actions are controlled by six sets of rules. These include the Washington Administrative Procedures Act, Washington Rules of Civil Procedure, Washington Rules of Appellate Procedure (RAP), the ABA Standards and the ODC Rules of Ethical Conduct and Procedure (ELCs and RPCs). Since it was an appeal, The Washington Rules of Appellate Procedure were the set most recently used during the first Bar Review before the board. The Washington RAPs give 30 days to file an appeal to the Supreme Court. I sent in my appeal 18 days after the review board findings were filed.

It was returned. As is turns out, Bar has its own special rule for appeals and only allows 15 days to file in the state Supreme Court. Other states allow up to 60 days.

The rules allowed the Washington Supreme Court to hear a discretionary appeal. The Bar rule wasn't jurisdictional.

The Washington Supreme Court refused to hear a discretionary appeal.

In response, I filed a second time in Federal Court to enjoin the entry of an order made without jurisdiction, venue and on the basis of illegally sequestered evidence. The federal court behaved peevishly and refused to hear the case. It abstained, despite the fact that Abstention requires an ongoing state proceeding and all proceedings were over. Abstention also requires a court to hold a case in abeyance until any state proceeding is over and hear it then, but the judge dismissed with prejudice. "With Prejudice" means the case can't be re-filed.

Abstention is a way for a court to avoid making a responsible statement while protecting its partisan relationships. Dismissing "with prejudice" is a way to bury an inconvenient truth.

When a party is disbarred, no other state will allow him to practice. It's a national ban. No employer will want a disbarred attorney because it carries a stigma of dishonesty. Any employment would be difficult.

The parties charged with maintaining standards of honesty used deceit to foil someone who acted to protect the legal system. ODC engaged the attorney who facilitated theft and accounting fraud against a 93 year old widow to foil the son who was protecting her. ODC used the corrupt tactics of a corrupt Cleveland administration to make sure the party who was exposing that corruption had no voice. ODC used bad arguments and rules against a party who insisted that all statutes and argument should take place at a high level.

This matter is currently in the 9th circuit. Perhaps a court sitting in California will be able to publicize the failures of Ohio which found a willing participant in Washington state.

21

The Fresh and Consistent Failures of Cleveland J. Michael Donnelly

Attorneys are sanctioned for conflicts of interest. They cannot be opposing counsel if they have represented an adverse party, or a relative of that party, or have worked for the firm which represented an adverse party in the past. Computer programs for identifying conflict relations have been generated. However, a substantial number of the judges in Cuyahoga County worked in the County Prosecutor's office prior to becoming County judges.

I hired an attorney to remove Ohio filing restrictions under ORC 2323.52 (vexatious litigator statute) against me. He filed a Civ. Rule 60/Declaratory Judgment action to have the restrictions declared void. The defendant was the Cuyahoga County Clerk of Courts. The case was assigned to a judge named Michael Donnelly who worked in the County Prosecutor's office under Bill Mason. Opposing counsel (the county prosecutor handles cases against the county) claimed I had to have filing permission from the judge who imposed the filing restriction in the first place. This was wrong. The Ohio Vexatious Litigator statute only restricts filing by unrepresented plaintiffs. The original judge (Lillian Greene) was no longer working. J. Lance Mason took over her docket.

I drove from Vermont for the Case Management conference. J. Donnelly was very friendly and had his staff attorney speak with Lance Mason's office. Permission to file was granted. It looked like a finished deal. We moved for Summary Judgment which would obviate the need for one. There was no legitimate reason to have a trial. I had won the case already. We just needed an order to finalize things.

J. Donnelly set a hearing for the Summary Judgment motion on April 20, 2013. He wanted all parties to attend. I had to drive from Vermont, again. Judges don't have you travel a long way when they are going to rule against you. Donnelly could have denied the Summary Judgment motion without a hearing.

But Donnelly managed to fail. Someone told him about me and my disfavored status in the state. When I arrived, he was peevish and said he was "losing patience". He refused to rule on the motion for Summary Judgment and wanted the case transferred to J. Mason, who "is very fair".

Donnelly had to hear the case. It was assigned to him by the administrative judge.   I just drove (another) 750 miles for what was certain to be a victory.

As of December, 2013, there has been no decision from J. Lance Mason. His staff attorney had not returned calls or written correspondence. ("This is the staff attorney for the Hon. J. Lance Mason. Please leave a message and I will return your call.")

Entities we cannot see are determining disposition of cases. Somebody or a group of somebodies presented a risk to Donnelly if he decided my case according to law. He could not jeopardize his career for what he perceived to be the obligations of his group.

A governor doesn't run a state. Prosecutors do.

Epilogue
Solutions for a Politicized Judiciary

Government and organized crime aren't that different. The idea is to get something for your group at the expense of people who aren't in it. The Jewish holocaust can be cast as not only racism, but a planned transfer of wealth. You kill the person you've cheated to remove his voice. Andrew Jackson did it with the Cherokee Indians after gold was found in Georgia. No one is innocent.

Politics is defined as competition for resources under conditions of scarcity. It's common for judiciaries to be politicized, especially in states where judges are elected. However, when the legal system charged with keeping your group together is politicized, it will discriminate in favor of itself at the expense of the people it's designed to protect. You will no longer have a national consensus. There will be higher priority people in the interest group and those outside. No one will trust government or the law and the "belief in belief" necessary to common endeavor will disappear. The country will subdivide into small interest groups and entities able to provide income for their constituents.

When the failures of Ohio find a willing participant among the banal and soggy residents of Washington state, we have to acknowledge that the mentality of our legal system has deteriorated on a national scale. Our jurisprudence of individual rights is being replaced with pragmatisms and income strategies.

Good people and bad people use the same rules; their intent differs. The presumption of legitimacy is being used by those in charge of legal administrations to behave dishonestly. Ohio has brought us to a point where it's possible to say that those who practice American Constitutional culture are a threat to the legal system because a culture of jurisprudence curtails individual license and income.

What to Do?

There are several things which can be done to improve state judiciaries.

First, they must be depoliticized. The states which choose judges by election only have the most gruesome record of judicial misconduct. See Ohio, Texas, Pennsylvania and Washington. Judges will favor parties who contribute to their campaigns. Adam Liptak of The NY Times did an article on Ohio Supreme Court J. Terence O'Donnell. He rules in favor of his contributors 91% of the time.

Second, judges must be rotated from jurisdiction to jurisdiction every 1-2 years. When judges sit in one location for a generation (elected judges tend to stay in office for as long as they want) they make preferred relations with local prosecutors, police, city administrators, attorneys and the district courts in the area. Moving judges from venue to venue makes extra-legal working arrangements difficult.

Third, Judges must be subject to public hearings prior to final elections. Those judges who survive a primary election, or who are submitted for appointment by a state procedure, must be scrutinized in public hearings where lay and professional testimony will be offered. These hearing would be announced in advance and anyone who wanted to testify in them would be scheduled at the hearing.

Fourth, judges must be subject to ongoing review every two years by a federal commission. It's bad enough that people choose judges without a sufficient data base, but the problem of job performance hasn't been sufficiently solved. Judge performance should be monitored during his/her time in office. All attorneys should be compelled to fill out short, multiple choice forms after a litigation is complete. The forms would include criteria such as knowledge of the law, impartiality, behavior towards litigants, evidence of psychiatric or cognitive disorder, evidence of substance abuse, ability to apply the law and work ethic. These forms would be collected and scored.

If a judge had below a certain score, he would be subject to a review committee. These forms and review committee proceedings would be public. The schedule of proceedings would be publicly announced, a month in advance, by internet and local printed media in an accessible location.

If a judge was found to be lacking in a particular area, he would be subject to sanctions/corrective remedies such as 1) continuing education in a particular area, 2) admonishment/warning, 3) probation for a period of 6 months to a year,

4) suspension (ranging from one day to several months), 5) removal from office, 6) referral to criminal justice system.

These results would be published within one week of a determination. Review determinations must be made within 30 days of a public hearing.

As stated above, judge review must be done by a body relatively independent of state and local politics. I suggest more federal involvement.

Fifth, Federal Judges should not be seated in the Federal District in which they were seated as state judges. All the partisan relations a judge makes while he's developing his career at the local and county level are carried to the Federal appointment. You end up with all the local biases and political alliances taking place in a different building in the same city or county....just on a higher and more destructive level.

About the Author

Robert Grundstein

Mr. Grundstein's pursuit of his interests has provided a good diversion from making a living. His education includes liberal arts at the University of Michigan, culinary training and a degree in piano performance. He has traveled on six continents and produced many articles, editorials, social commentaries and books. The subject matter of his works include public affairs, travel, food and the culture of food.

Under duress, he will admit he went to law school and is a state bar member, but found a dignified way to make a living.

He also loves hockey and is sure he'll be drafted real soon.

Made in the USA
San Bernardino, CA
09 October 2015